BLONDE
AMBITION

BLONDE AMBITION

THE UNTOLD STORY BEHIND ANNA NICOLE SMITH'S DEATH

BY

Rita Cosby

GRAND CENTRAL
PUBLISHING

NEW YORK   BOSTON

Grand Central Publishing
Hachette Book Group USA
237 Park Avenue
New York, NY 10017

Visit our Web site at www.HachetteBookGroupUSA.com.

Printed in the United States of America

First Edition: September 2007
10 9 8 7 6 5

Grand Central Publishing is a division of Hachette Book Group USA, Inc. The Grand Central Publishing name and logo is a trademark of Hachette Book Group USA, Inc.

ISBN-10: 0-446-40611-2
ISBN-13: 978-0-446-40611-6
LCCN: 2007929808

Text design and composition by Ellen Rosenblatt/SDDesigns

Contents

Author's Note

IN 2007, I WAS THE FIRST TO BREAK THE OFFICIAL NEWS TO THE world that Anna Nicole Smith was dead. At the time, I was a journalist with NBC. Hours after the tragic news came down, I was on plane after plane, following the story back and forth from Florida to the Bahamas. As a seasoned host and reporter, I've covered infamous manhunts, murder trials, and met with saints and sinners all over the globe. I've talked personally to Pope John Paul II and peeled back the "truth" from Scott Peterson and Oklahoma City bomber Timothy McVeigh.

But nothing could've prepared me for the chaos and media frenzy surrounding the story that is Anna Nicole. As the continuing drama has unfolded, I've talked to hundreds of people connected to the case. Sometimes nothing is as it seems. What you saw on television was a far cry from what was really happening behind closed doors. This is that story.

Preface

VICKIE LYNN MARSHALL, BETTER KNOWN TO THE MILLIONS OF people worldwide as Anna Nicole Smith, took her last breath at the Hard Rock Hotel in Hollywood, Florida, on February 8th, 2007 in room 607. That much is certain.

But beyond that there exists a deceptive web of conflicting stories, misdirection, tragic mistakes, and an illusion of truth among a host of unwitting yet willing partners. The death of the former stripper turned reality star is as perplexing as her life.

This is the story of untold secrets. It proves that truth is stranger than fiction, and reality is sometimes unreal.

BLONDE
AMBITION

CHAPTER 1

Timing Is Everything

JUST AFTER 1 P.M. ON FEBRUARY 8, 2007, BRIGITTE NEVEN NO-
ticed that Anna Nicole Smith's chest wasn't rising and falling
like a normal sleeping person. Something wasn't right. In fact,
something was terribly wrong, which Brigitte soon realized
when she tried to shut Anna's agape jaw and it wouldn't close.
It was stiff.

Brigitte Neven is, in fact, the woman who actually found
Anna Nicole Smith's lifeless body. The story you might have
heard was that she was discovered unconscious by her "private nurse." Brigitte is not a nurse. There was a nurse in the
room, Tasma Brighthaupt, wife of Anna's bodyguard, Maurice "Big Moe" Brighthaupt, but "Tas" was at the foot of Anna's king size bed, intently working on her computer, unaware
of the deadly silence lying in the bed behind her. This day, like
many in the previous few months in the life of the woman
who was famous for being famous, would be spent in bed.

Anna Nicole Smith had a routine: she would start her day

1

with a shot around 9 a.m. of "longevity drugs"—a varying combination of vitamin B12, immunoglobulins, and human growth hormone. The combination of drugs is said to maintain energy, decrease body fat and improve mood and motivation. She'd then go back to bed and sleep into the afternoon, wake up, eat something, drink something, take something, watch a little TV, and sleep some more. Then, repeat. The last few years, and in particular the last few months since the death of her beloved son Daniel, her life was an endless cycle of depression and sadness, blurred and numbed by a dangerous combination of drugs and alcohol.

But this day was unlike the others. Something had happened. Something had pushed the voluptuous beauty over the edge. And now she was free-falling from the living to the dead.

Three days earlier, Monday, February 5

In advance of Anna and Howard's arrival in Florida, Moe received several packages in the mail addressed to Howard as he had on other occasions when Anna and Howard were expected. Private investigators hired by an interested party told me that Moe said he received the packages at his house, addressed from the husband of Anna's friend/psychiatrist Dr. Khristine Eroshevich, who was traveling with Anna from the Bahamas. Moe noted that labels on the boxes indicated they came from a pharmacy, and on Monday night, he gave the packages to Howard at the Hard Rock.

That morning, before their trip to Florida, Anna had started the day with a dance lesson in the Bahamas to prepare for an upcoming event and music video for TrimSpa, the diet supplement for which she was the paid spokesmodel. Anna called Mrs. Gerlene Gibson, the go-to woman in the Bahamas if you're a celebrity and have babysitting needs. She asked her to come to the house and take care of five-month-old Dannielynn for a few days. Gerlene Gibson is the mother of Shane Gibson, the Bahamian Minister of Immigration, who had helped Anna secure her permanent residency in the Bahamas.

After hugging Mrs. Gibson and kissing Dannielynn goodbye, Anna was driven to the airport and boarded an afternoon flight to Florida, along with Dr. Khristine Eroshevich and Howard K. Stern, her lawyer and the man publicly claiming to be the father of her newborn. According to statements taken by Broward County medical examiner, Dr. Joshua Perper, Anna was upbeat and feeling well, looking forward to shopping for a few days in Florida before picking up a newly purchased boat and returning to the Bahamas later in the week.

Anna began to complain about pain in her left buttock during the flight to Florida. The spot was tender from one of her daily injections. Since Anna's pain was in her left buttock and Anna was right-handed, it would be highly unlikely and extremely difficult for her to have given herself the shot. But later, when asked by Dr. Perper, neither Howard Stern nor Dr. Eroshevich would admit giving it to her. And Dr. Perper wouldn't ask twice.

• • •

During the limousine ride from the Miami International Airport, Anna complained of feeling cold and of increasing buttock pain. By the time they arrived at the Hard Rock Hotel, Anna was woozy.

She had been to the Hard Rock the month before, in January 2007, when she made her first high profile public appearance since her son's death. Anna had put on her celebrity face, shaded seductively in over-sized, high-glam sunglasses, and joined the star-studded crowd for a Don King produced boxing match, televised live on Showtime. Seated near ringside at the Hard Rock, with other notables such as wrestling star Hulk Hogan, actor Mickey Rourke, and hoops legend Shaquille O'Neal, Anna took in the fight while companion Howard K. Stern snapped shots on his ever-present digital camera. Besides new blonde extensions, zinged with pink highlights, Anna wore a slinky beaded black top, which showcased her voluptuous figure and shoulder tattoo.

Since shooting a commercial at the Hard Rock Hotel for the TrimSpa Million Dollar Makeover Challenge, Anna was a celebrity "regular" at the hotel, which meant her $1600 a night suite was often compliments of the house. In the commercial, she had jiggled left and right in front of the Hard Rock sign while cooing such lines as "Want to step into my reality?" and "Like my body?" Ending, of course, with her unforgettable hustle "TrimSpa, baby!"

While everyone might not be an Anna Nicole fan, one thing everyone agreed upon was that Anna Nicole Smith knew how to get noticed.

But what hotel guests noticed on that clear Monday night in February, as she arrived with Howard and Dr. Khris, was that she couldn't even get her foot out of the limo. She got stuck, and Howard had to physically help her out and then assist her upstairs. "She's been at the hotel a number of times," a hotel employee told me, "but this time was different. She was spacey, unusually weird."

She and Howard checked in at 8:10 p.m. under "Fred and Wilma Flintstone," their usual not-so-discrete codeword for "I'm-a-celebrity." Hotel employees said Howard kept her from talking to people and told everyone she had the flu. They went up to room 607, accompanied by Dr. Khris, and another male. Anna's "Florida person," bodyguard "Big Moe" Brighthaupt, joined them later. He brought with him the packages he received from his house, which, according to statements he provided to private investigators, he soon learned contained prescriptions that Howard K. Stern was expecting for their stay in Florida.

Room 607, known as a "Fillmore Suite," is the second door on the left off the elevators, right past the display of Tori Amos memorabilia in the hotel's south tower. Room 607 has one bedroom, a living room area, and one and a half baths. In total, 750 square feet. They also had the room next door, room 609, connected to 607 by a door that locks on both sides. Room 609 is a "deluxe room" with two beds.

Hotel workers say Anna and Howard often partied in their room during prior visits with what they believe was cocaine and that both were often heard sniffling and cleaning up "stuff" around the room when hotel staff came in, while others saw white powder on the counters. But this week was different. After check-in, room 607 went into lockdown. Bellhops, housekeeping, and room service were all met at the door. Hotel employees were not allowed into the room. Period. Once Anna was carried over the threshold of room 607 that Monday night, she wasn't seen again in public until she was wheeled out on a gurney.

• • •

When Anna got into the room, she was very sick and shivering uncontrollably. Dr. Khris called the hotel staff and asked them to order a prescription for ten 75 mg capsules of Tamiflu (an antiviral agent) and Ciprofloxacin (a potent antibiotic, prescribed as an antidote during the anthrax scare shortly after 9/11). Although Dr. Khris told hotel employees that she had been Anna's "personal nurse" for years, she said that she wasn't able to prescribe in the United States. At first, she requested that the hotel's doctor write the prescription that she felt Anna needed—a strange request given the fact that she had been prescribing medications to Anna for years from various American pharmacies. Eventually, both prescriptions were called in to the local Walgreens Pharmacy using Dr. Khris' name as the doctor, but the medications weren't listed under the name Anna Nicole Smith. Instead, the medications were prescribed for "Alex Katz," a non-hotel guest.

Alex Katz, a 60-year-old south Floridian businessman, whom I later learned to be a friend of Dr. Khris's, was with them that night and actually picked up at least one prescription, while a hotel concierge picked up a thermometer. Normally, the concierge can pick up prescriptions, but in this case, Anna's party insisted on getting the prescription themselves. When I contacted Alex Katz, he confirmed his friendship with Dr. Khris, but quickly told me, "I don't want to talk about that night" and hung up. A source close to the investigation says Katz later refused to talk to Seminole Police and "lawyered up and shut up quickly."

That night was apparently messy. According to Anna's bodyguard Moe's early interviews with news media, he said that he took Anna's temperature and when it registered a startling 105 degrees, he told her she needed to go to the hospital. Moe, a trained paramedic, threatened Anna that he was going to call an ambulance. He said in a February 26, 2007, interview broadcast on Greta Van Susteren's Fox News television show that he told Anna that her decision not to go to the hospital was unacceptable. "You can get upset with me and we don't talk for a week if you want. That's fine," he told the shivering beauty. "But my goal is to make sure you're healthy."

Moe has said privately that surprisingly no one else was really pushing Anna to go to the hospital, especially Dr. Khris. "It wasn't like she was discouraging her," he noted, "but she was definitely not encouraging her." Moe thought this was highly unusual for someone with a medical background, even though she, like him, wasn't there for the paycheck. He made note that neither he nor Dr. Khris was serving in a paid capacity.

Apparently, none of them wanted to argue with Anna to make her go to the hospital, not her medically trained friends or her live-in lawyer Howard K. Stern. Howard said in a statement his attorneys released shortly after Anna's death that he thought Anna would be alive today if she hadn't refused medical help. He said that he had urged Anna to check into a hospital after her spike in temperature, but that she refused because "she did not want the media frenzy that follows her."

So, Anna didn't go to the hospital; instead, Moe claims he picked her up and put her naked body into the deep whirlpool tub of the master-bathroom. It was filled with ice cubes and cold water. Anna's fever broke, dropping a dramatic eight degrees. The medical examiner questioned Dr. Khris, but didn't ask who specifically gave her the medications, or why Anna was given two tablespoons of chloral hydrate, a potent 19th century sleep aid, even though the recommended dosage is two *tea*spoons. Interestingly, chloral hydrate was a contributing factor to both Anna's demise as well as the death of her idol, Marilyn Monroe.

Anna Nicole Smith fell asleep on the first night of her last week alive around 10 p.m.

Tuesday, February 6

Anna Nicole awoke the following morning with a temperature of 100 degrees and was vomiting and had diarrhea. The medical examiner's office would later report that throughout the day on Tuesday she did not urinate and had a "pungent" odor. She did, however, feel good enough to watch television, an encouraging sign to Howard, Dr. Khris, and Moe. In the afternoon, under the supervision of Dr. Khris, she took a bath and drank various fluids including Fiji water, chamomile tea, and Pedialyte, a formula typically used for infants to prevent dehydration. The medical examiner's report also says she "was given" chloral hydrate and slept for two hours. When she awoke, she watched television until 11 p.m. at which time "she took" another unusually large dose of chloral hydrate and went to sleep. There is no explanation in the report as to why Anna was first routinely "given" the chloral hydrate and then suddenly "took" it herself as the week went on.

Wednesday, February 7

Howard, Khris, and Moe report that Anna was awake in bed watching television around 11 a.m. For lunch, she was feeling good enough to eat an egg white and spinach omelet, but by afternoon, she had taken a turn for the worse. According to statements given by Howard and Dr. Khris to the medical examiner, Anna was found that afternoon sitting in the dry bathtub, naked and confused. She then took a bath and, feeling slightly better, ordered two crab cakes and shrimp for dinner from room service who left the food on a cart by the door to the suite.

In the evening, Anna became very upset when Dr. Khristine had to leave for California. Anna began complaining about not feeling well. She begged Dr. Khris not to go, but Dr. Khris said she had to get back to her private practice in Los Angeles. Dr. Khris, Anna's psychiatrist, was also Anna's next-door neighbor. Anna told one of her good friends, Jackie Hatten, that she loved having a psychiatrist that she could talk to every day, "just like Marilyn Monroe did."

After Dr. Khris left, Moe stayed the night in room 609, the other bedroom of the suite. "It was an open room, and I knew she wasn't feeling well," Moe said in the Fox News interview. "And Howard just asked me, 'Hey, can you just stay over?' I said, 'Oh, no problem.'"

According to a source close to the investigation, there was one problem for Moe when police later looked at the Hard Rock Hotel's surveillance tapes. What the public doesn't know is that there was someone else in the suite the night before Anna died. That night, Moe was seen walking into the suite with a mysterious woman. A woman that wasn't his wife.

Thursday, February 8

Whether because of the insanity of the day—or the confusion of trying to keep a story straight—the times that certain things occurred on the day Anna died get blurry among all those involved. But there are two specific times that can't be denied. The first call for help came from room 607 at 1:38 p.m., and Anna Nicole Smith was pronounced dead at Memorial Regional Hospital at 2:49 p.m. It's what occurred before, during, and after that is troubling.

Big Moe has said that when he arrived back at the hotel the

night before—sometime between eight and ten o'clock—Anna was on the couch in the living room of the suite watching television and Howard was in the master bedroom. According to Moe, Anna was no longer on the couch at 4 a.m. According to the Broward County Medical Examiner's report, it is believed Anna Nicole took chloral hydrate before falling asleep the night before. Howard told investigators he slept in bed with her and when she awoke around 9 a.m. he said she did not complain of pain, but felt very weak and asked him to help her get to the bathroom and back to bed.

Howard K. Stern also made a point to tell Seminole Police that he did not give Anna any medication that day and he told them that he "did not see her take medication, but believed she was taking her medication." Moe said he came into the room that morning sometime around 9 a.m. to tell Howard he was going to go have breakfast with his wife, Tas, and would be back shortly. Moe told the police that he "thought" he saw Anna moving in bed that morning, but later, when he discussed the morning with others, he said that Anna received medicine from Howard around 9 a.m. "like she always did."

But Moe says something was peculiar that morning. Howard's behavior.

At 10:45 a.m., Moe and Tas were waiting for the breakfast they ordered at the hotel restaurant when Moe's phone rang. It was Howard asking if Moe would mind going to the airport to pick up King Eric when he arrived. Seventy-three-year-old King Eric Gibson, the former husband of Mrs. Gerlene Gibson and father to Shane Gibson, is the Bahamian boat captain who was going to pilot Anna's new boat back to the Bahamas. Moe said he and Tas would go pick them up.

According to Tas's subsequent statements to private investigators, Howard called again a few minutes later to say it was time to go pick up King Eric and his party. "Howard wanted to stay with Anna because she was so sick," Tas said. Since she and Moe had planned to do some errands, Tas wondered aloud who was going to go to the boat.

"No way Howard is going to leave Anna," Moe said to Tas over breakfast. "No way he'll go to the boat." They decided King Eric and his boat hand could go alone then and they could still get to their errands as planned.

After picking up King Eric, his sixty-three-year-old common-law wife, Brigitte Neven, and King Eric's first mate at the airport, Moe and Tas brought them back to the Hard Rock a little before noon. They were waiting at the elevator bank to go up to the room when Howard came out of the elevator they were about to get into. Tas says he was "fidgety, strange acting" and that "he seemed surprised when he saw us."

"What's up?" Moe asked.

"I just came down to use my cell phone," Howard said.

"Why?" Moe asked. "It works just fine in the room."

Howard stuttered. "Ah, ah."

According to Tas, "He didn't say anything, and then just went upstairs in the elevator with all of us." When she thinks back on the day, she said, "I still cannot get over his behavior at that moment."

The entire group walked into Room 609 and Tas says Howard was "talking in a normal, in a loud voice, which in hindsight seems strange given that Anna was supposed to be sleeping. He wasn't whispering." He shouted out to Anna, saying, "Anna we have guests." Also, Howard did something that in retrospect seems "calculated," Tas says. "He stood in front of the living room area in between the two rooms, with his back to the master bedroom. So we could barely look into 607." Tas also recalled it was "like he was intentionally blocking our view of Anna inside the next room."

They were only in the room for a few minutes when Howard announced the boat appointment was at noon. "Noon?" King Eric asked. "It's twelve o'clock now."

"Oh," Howard said. "Then, we have to go."

Moe was surprised Howard said he was going to leave and asked, "Who's going to look after Anna?"

"Brigitte will look after Anna," Howard said.

Moe didn't like the idea of Brigitte staying alone with Anna when she was so sick, so he asked Tas to stay too. "Just stay for a little while, baby," he said. "Do you mind?"

Tas shrugged her shoulders and said, "Okay." Moe then told her she could take his computer and check her e-mails. Tas told private investigators that she was surprised about staying "since the plan was for me to do errands, not to baby-sit Anna."

Moe told the private investigators he thought it was strange that "at first Howard didn't want to leave her, but it was okay to leave her later?" Numerous people who are familiar with the relationships told me that both Howard and Moe leaving Anna while she was so sick was highly unusual. Typically, one or both would stay by her side. But the men all left the suite, leaving three women behind—the bodyguard's wife, the boat captain's companion, and Anna Nicole Smith, the world famous beauty, in bed and in trouble.

The strange thing about Howard's noon appointment was that it wasn't at noon at all. "Howard had a one o'clock appointment with me," the boat handyman told me. "Definitely one o'clock."

According to Mark Dekema, the yacht broker from "Reel Deal Yachts" who had sold Anna the boat in January for a little less than the advertised price of $129,000, Howard called several times during the week to reschedule the appointment. The Thursday appointment to inspect the boat had been origanally scheduled for Tuesday but Howard had called on Monday to say that he needed to postpone a day because both he and Anna had "the stomach flu." Tuesday, he postponed again, but said, "Let's definitely make it Thursday." There were approximately five or six calls between the two men on Thursday, but Dekema said the time was always set for one o'clock. "Howard seemed normal," Dekema said. "Like an excited boat buyer."

• • •

Back at the Hard Rock, Tasma Brighthaupt and Brigitte Neven were getting acquainted in the luxury suite. Brigitte began thumbing through the promotional materials in the room. What she really wanted to do was go down where the hotel was gearing up for its annual Seminole Tribal Fair Powwow in which Native Americans stroll the halls in brightly colored attire, and hotel guests and busloads of schoolchildren learn about Native American culture and food. Brigitte was hungry. She hadn't eaten since early that morning before they left the Bahamas. But soon the two women realized they couldn't leave the room. Neither Brigitte nor Tas were left with a room key, and they needed a key to get past security at the elevators. So, if they went downstairs, they couldn't get back up. They were stuck in the suite.

The two women made small talk. Tas is Bahamian and grew up in Nassau. Brigitte, who has spent her adult life in the Bahamas, grew up in Germany. Tas is a trained nurse, having gotten her license a little more than a year before, in December 2005. Brigitte said she loved the Bahamas, its people, the weather, and the food . . . Food. Brigitte was really hungry, so she pulled out the room service menu and ordered up some food. Tas began working on her computer. A little while later, as Brigitte read a book, Tas said she was having problems with her computer, so she went into the bedroom where Anna slept, to the foot of the king size bed and used the computer on a table there.

• • •

Anna's new boat, a 39-foot 1995 Carver, had been paid for by wire transfer on January 19, and she had already christened it *The Cracker*, a name she used to call herself and her son, a tongue-in-cheek term for a white person living in a black community. The boat was ready and waiting at the Royal Palm Yacht Basin in Dania, Florida, directly south of the Ft. Lauderdale Airport, six miles east of the Hard Rock Hotel.

Though Anna had wanted to make the entire interior pink, her favorite color, boat broker Mark Dekema says he talked Howard out of this, giving them estimates of the retrofitting changes they wanted of between $16,000 and $22,000. All of which Howard said was too high. Instead, they settled on adding two big screen TV's, including a 36" flat screen in the master salon.

Howard wasn't late for a noon appointment; he was early for a one o'clock appointment. When the handyman got to the boat basin promptly at 1 p.m., Howard and King Eric were waiting for him. The handyman, who had done the minor repairs and upgrades and had also managed the boat for the previous owner, greeted them and took them to the boat. The boat was scheduled to be put in the water later that day and was already in the lift, a crane-like mechanism that lowers boats into the water. The men climbed aboard and began looking around, and the handyman pointed out things about the boat as they went. The boat has two private staterooms, comfortable seating for six, and a wet bar with an icemaker, ideal for entertaining.

The handyman said he spoke about the boat for ten or so minutes, during which time Howard seemed very detached, only giving one-word answers and comments. "He was cold," the handyman told me. "He showed no emotion at all." The handyman told me he was surprised that Howard himself even came for the appointment, noting that the things to check could have been easily done by his captain, King Eric.

Right about 1:15 p.m. Howard was on his cell phone with Mark Dekema, the boat salesman; Dekema wanted to make sure everything was okay.

● ● ●

Things weren't okay back at the Hard Rock, even though, according to Tas, only five minutes prior she told Moe that they were. Shortly after 1:00 p.m., Moe had called his wife from his cell phone to talk about his errands and check on how Anna was doing. He originally told the media it was about fifteen minutes after he left the Hard Rock for a "twenty minute errand," but it had been, as we now know, at least an hour after all the men left the suite.

"How's she doing?" Moe asked.

"She's still sleeping," his wife told him as she worked on the computer, Anna lying in the bed behind her.

"Okay," he said, ending the call so he could continue running his errands.

Brigitte, hearing conversation in the master bedroom, thought that Anna had finally awoken, so she came into the room to say hello. The room was dark, completely veiled from sunny southern Florida. There was a light on in the bathroom, but the only light in the room was the glow of Tas's computer screen and the television broadcasting an afternoon soap opera, whose most dramatic moment could never surpass the chaos that was about to ensue in room 607.

"Please don't wake up Anna," Tas whispered to Brigitte. Brigitte realized that Tas was on her cell phone, not talking to Anna.

Brigitte didn't think sleeping into the afternoon this long was normal. She had spent the last few months in the Bahamas trying to bring Anna back to life again after her son Daniel's tragic, untimely death that was still clouded by many more questions than answers. Brigitte and her companion, King Eric Gibson, had befriended the depressed Anna, taking her out on King Eric's boat and cooking for her Bahamian style. Anna loved King Eric's fried fish, and the couple liked being with Anna. On her good days, they found her to be "adorable and childlike."

Brigitte would bring Anna out of the sheltered, overly air-conditioned house for a boat ride or a walk on the beach. When they went out on the boat, Anna was happy, as happy and carefree as someone in her circumstances could be. Life for Anna hadn't been easy of late, if ever. She had lost her son three days after giving birth to her daughter in September; she was in the midst of a nasty custody feud over her newborn with Larry Birkhead, a former boyfriend claiming to be the father of her child; she was in the throes of a ten-year messy legal battle over her dead octogenarian husband's billion dollar estate; and she had mounting bills, user friends, troubles with her family, and the bane of her existence, her ever-fluctuating weight.

Brigitte delighted in bringing out Anna's childlike exuberance, in pulling her up from the depths of depression and getting her to do things she'd never done. She always brought baby Dannielynn along. Dannielynn loved the rocking of the boat. She'd smile a big toothless grin and open her big blue eyes wide with excitement. It did not go unnoticed that neither she nor her mother ever cried on these boat trips. They'd find the perfect spot near a secluded beach, anchor the boat, and carry the baby through the water high above their heads to the beach. Brigitte would put on her snorkel and mask and dive for seashells, presenting Anna with the most beautiful ones.

Anna began calling King Eric and Brigitte "Mommy" and "Daddy" shortly after she came to know them. They could see she was searching for something, something that she told them she never really had. She longed for family, for love, for someone she could lean on and trust. She was always happy to be a part of whatever Brigitte and King Eric were doing, whether it was boating or going to listen to King Eric play his steel drums at a club, as he is a famous musician known throughout the islands.

Perhaps it was the day watching her first Bahamian Regatta that Anna decided she was going to buy a boat. Rather than standing on shore, Brigitte took her out on a boat to watch the experience up close. Brigitte let Anna take the wheel. "Let's go up with Daddy," Anna giggled mischievously. "Let's go up with Daddy, I want him to see me drive the boat." She maneuvered the boat near King Eric's racing sloop, *Lucayan Lady*. "Look!" she screamed to him across the water. "I'm driving the boat!"

The plan for the week of February 8 was that the six of them—King Eric at the helm, his first mate, Brigitte, Howard, Anna, and Moe—would sail back to the Bahamas. But this plan had somehow gone terribly awry.

• • •

Back at the Hard Rock when Brigitte quietly approached Anna's bed, she noticed she could barely see her. Anna was bundled up in a heavy down comforter. Only a few strands of her blonde hair were visible. Brigitte moved the comforter back from her face. "Come here," Brigitte said to Tas as she stared at Anna's lifeless body. "You gotta come here! Something is wrong."

"What do you mean?" Tas asked, walking around the four-poster king size bed.

"Something is wrong," Brigitte said, pointing at Anna's face. "Look!" Tas pulled the thick comforter and white striped duvet farther down. Anna was lying on her right side and right shoulder, facing the left wall, atop soft Egyptian cotton sheets. She was naked. Friends and former boyfriends of Anna's told me that her sleeping in the nude was very strange—that Anna never slept in the nude, that she always wore a top and panties when she slept, and usually a bra to give her additional support even when she was sick. In fact, friends say she was obsessed with buying oversized t-shirts to sleep in. Besides comfort, there was also a vanity issue for Anna. Even though she was known for her voluptuous figure, she had several botched plastic surgeries, one of which scarred her left nipple leaving it quite deformed. Because of this they say she would never have been totally undressed, especially with people coming in and out of the hotel room. It is one of the many details that doesn't seem right about the scene in room 607 that day. But what the two women saw wasn't just not right, it was downright frightening. Anna Nicole's trademark pink lips had drained of color. They were now a pale blue.

"Wake up, Anna!" Tas screamed, shaking Anna's naked body. "Wake up!" She rolled her onto her back. Anna's overly enhanced breasts flopped to opposite sides of her chest. The two women, who had only known each other for a little more than an hour, together began to try to resuscitate the lifeless body of Anna Nicole Smith.

Tas ran into the bathroom to get some water. Brigitte says she hoped there was a "flicker of life still left," but quickly realized there was "nothing that we could do for her." They splashed Anna's face with water. No response. They put a mirror beneath her nose to see if there was any breath. There wasn't. The former Playboy Playmate was in dire straights.

"We were so busy," Brigitte told me. "We wanted to try—we still believed we could—you know, somehow. We yelled at her . . . it was terrible."

According to an interview Tas did with *Entertainment Tonight,* she hit the button on her earpiece "because my husband was the last person I spoke to and that would ring back to his phone." She told private investigators that when she got Moe on the phone she told him right away, "I don't like what I'm seeing. Anna has purple splotches on her face and body. She's not breathing and looks blue."

"She's blue?" Moe asked.

"You need to get back here," she said. "And you need to call 911." She told investigators that when she blew air into Anna, "I heard a gurgling sound and I told Moe I knew it was not good."

Tas told private investigators that her husband said, "Don't do anything, I'll be right there. Don't worry, I'll handle it." He also told his wife he'd call 911. But he didn't. Who he called was Howard.

• • •

It has been reported that when Howard got the call from Moe—right after Moe learned from his wife that Anna wasn't breathing—Howard was still on the dry-docked boat in the marina talking on his cell phone to boat salesman Mark Dekema. He interrupted the conversation with an abrupt, "I have another call. I gotta take this." Dekema says Howard sounded urgent, "a little desperate," with an "edge of concern" in his voice.

"Howard," Moe said, "you got to get back. Something's wrong with Anna." Moe later said that Howard was in disbelief. His only response was, "Oh, okay."

"Just get back," Moe told him.

According to Moe, rather than calling 911 directly, the next thing he did was call the hotel liaison because, as Moe told Fox News, "My phone is registered in Dade, my cell phone is registered in Dade [County]. I knew if I dialed 911 then possibly Dade rescue would pick up, and I didn't know the address to the Hard Rock, so I had our liaison that helped us out in the Hard Rock call 911. Then, I rushed back."

The only problem with that is . . . it isn't true.

According to the Federal Communications Commission, more than thirty percent of all 911 calls come from cell phones and the call is answered typically by a central operator in the city you are calling from, who can then immediately redirect the call if necessary to any area's emergency response team. Surprising naivety for Moe, a certified paramedic and a celebrity bodyguard. Also, Moe said he didn't know the address to the hotel, yet hotel employees say he had been there at least six times before. But what makes Moe's story especially disconcerting is that the call for help from room 607 didn't come until 1:38 p.m., many minutes later, around the time he had gotten back to the hotel. And he wasn't the one who made the call.

• • •

Meanwhile, Brigitte and Tas were trying anything and everything to revive Anna. "Anna!" Brigitte screamed as she began vigorously rubbing and tweaking Anna's feet while Tas climbed onto the bed and began attempting CPR on Anna's naked, unconscious body. Tas, a trained nurse, began vainly pushing against the springs of the mattress beneath Anna's body, not against an unmovable surface like a hard floor, as is necessary for CPR. "Anna! What's going to happen to your daughter?" Brigitte cried out. "You can't . . ." Brigitte was in shock and can't remember if the word "die" escaped her lips, but she knew the situation was critical.

Anna's body was still warm, but Tas told Brigitte there was no pulse. She peeled back the comatose beauty's eyelids. She said she thought there might have been a reaction in Anna's hazel eyes. "Anna, Anna!" Brigitte pleaded. "Wake up, Mommy is here!" Then, she prayed out loud: "Thy will be done."

As they struggled to save her, there was no struggle from Anna, no throwing up, nothing like that. Anna was just lying there. "We are so powerless when something happens to you," Brigitte told me later. "We think we can do something, but in reality, we can't really. You can do A, B, and C, but you can only do what you can do. I knew there was nothing that I really could do, but I do Reiki [a spiritual Japanese technique in which the healer does a "laying on of hands" to promote healing]. I began doing Reiki over Anna's body, and I sort of had this feeling that it was over, but I cannot say that because it's not for me to say. I got the feeling she was saying goodbye."

21

As the two women tired themselves in their efforts to revive Anna Nicole Smith, they realized that there was nothing they could do for her. She needed medical help urgently. *Where was the ambulance?* Brigitte thought. *It seems like it's taking forever.*

It wasn't taking forever. The ambulance had yet to be called.

•   •   •

Moe rushed back to the hotel. In early interviews, he said he was about fifteen minutes away and frantically ran every light to get there.

According to the handyman who was seated on the boat right across from Howard when he got the fateful call from Moe, the conversation lasted maybe one to two minutes at the most. And he said that Howard said only a few words to Moe, something to the effect of "Oh, okay, I'm on my way." Howard's first visible reaction when he got the news that all was not well with Anna could be described as surprising by some. "It didn't seem like an upsetting call to him at all," the handyman told me. "Which is odd to me, especially after I learned that the call was giving the bad news about her health." After Howard ended his call, he said in a monotone, unemotional voice, "I have an emergency and have to leave."

"He did not come across like it was a crisis at all," the handyman told me. "He didn't seem distressed. He was very matter of fact, like it was a minor business issue versus a personal crisis. It certainly didn't come across like it was a major emergency in any way. He acted very nonchalant."

In fact, after Howard got the call, the handyman says Howard answered several questions for him, including a conversation about whether Howard could pay him the few hundred dollars he owed him for the minor repairs he did. Howard said he forgot to bring the money. Howard then said goodbye and walked back to the car. "He definitely wasn't running or rushing to his car," the handyman said. "Just going through the paces, it seemed." It's approximately a three to four minute walk to where his car was parked from where the boat was docked. About ten minutes after the phone call, the handyman says the Town Car pulled out of the parking lot. In retrospect now knowing what Howard was told on the phone, the handyman described Howard's behavior as "extremely odd."

•   •   •

According to police records and hotel surveillance footage:

At 1:38 p.m., Tas was exhausted from her efforts and frustrated that help hadn't arrived. She called the hotel operator and said Anna Nicole was unconscious and needed emergency assistance immediately.

Within minutes, hotel security personnel were in the room. The Hard Rock Hotel is in the city of Hollywood, but it's actually located on tribal land, owned by the Seminole Indians, who have jurisdiction over all activities on their property. They are considered a sovereign nation on sovereign land, and only federal agents who work for the Bureau of Indian Affairs have authority on that land. Although Hollywood authorities assisted in the case, Seminole officials controlled the investigation and determined what information came in or out.

At 1:40 p.m., Hard Rock security called the Seminole Police Dispatch, and the Seminole Police called Seminole Rescue teams and Hollywood Fire and Rescue: "Hi, this is the Seminole Police," a female said on the recording of the 911 call. "If you could please respond to the Hard Rock, room 607. It is going to be in reference to a white female who is—what is she, not responsive? —She is not breathing and she is not responsive. She is actually Anna Nicole Smith. . . ."

• • •

Though Moe told police he was in the room and instructed his wife to call 911, eyewitnesses say that Moe arrived at the hotel and broke into a sprint across the hotel lobby, yelling toward the front desk to "Call 911!" According to surveillance tapes, he arrived in the room at 1:40, after the call for help had already finally been initiated.

When he arrived in the room, his wife was on top of Anna, continuing her unfruitful attempts to revive her. He moved her out of the way and felt for a pulse. He later said he might have felt a faint pulse. His first reaction was to pick Anna up and put her on the floor so he could properly do CPR on her. "When I had my lips around her lips, blowing," Moe said in an interview with Larry King, "blowing, breathing life, breathing air in her, and it blew back, I just . . . deep down . . . I just figured that she was going to, you know, see her son Daniel."

1:44 p.m. Seminole Police were on the scene.

1:47 p.m. Both Seminole Rescue and Hollywood Fire and Rescue arrived in the hotel room. They took over administering CPR and began ACLS protocol (Advance Cardiac Life Support), which included medications such as atropine (to try to jumpstart her heart), Narcan (a reversing agent in case she overdosed on narcotics), and they intubated her by inserting a breathing tube into her lungs and blowing oxygen directly into her lungs, but the air immediately blew right back out.

Later that day, Captain Dan Fitzgerald with the Hollywood Fire and Rescue Department would say, "There was just no way of knowing how long she'd been down before she was discovered, which could make all the difference in the world. If you witness somebody pass out, you can initiate care immediately. But if somebody passes out and it's not witnessed, they can be there for twenty minutes or so before they're found, it makes it a much more difficult scenario to work our protocols and be successful."

At 1:51 p.m., Howard K. Stern burst into the room, but was stopped by security personnel. According to King Eric, he had been stoic and quiet on the approximately fifteen-minute car ride back from the boat basin. "He didn't say anything," King Eric said. "He wasn't calm. He was fidgety. He didn't know what to do. At that point, we thought she just collapsed. I thought maybe she didn't eat or something." But when Howard got back to the hotel in front of a crowd of eyewitnesses, his response was much more heightened. He was seen running through the hotel and was very upset, quite different from his initial response when he received the call at the boat basin.

Room 607 had become a very hectic scene. Moe has said Howard was emotional and everyone was trying to calm him down. He asked, "Moe, is Anna all right?"

"She's in good hands," Moe said, referring to the slew of emergency personnel in the room.

Hotel surveillance tapes show Howard in the hallway, throwing his arms up and down and pacing feverishly in a circle. An emergency official at the scene told me Howard said, "I can't believe it." At first, he was not crying, but mumbling to himself, hitting his leg in disbelief. One eyewitness told me, "It wasn't like he was in mourning or sad. He wasn't grieving, it was more panicking."

"Don't go!" Howard shouted into the room at Anna's body. "Stay!" Brigitte hugged him and she remembers him screaming out, "Ah, Anna! Without you I'm nothing!"

Approximately 2:15 p.m., it was Moe, rather than Howard, who ran beside the gurney carrying the tabloid icon to the waiting ambulance below. Eyewitnesses say Howard ran down the hallway following the gurney up to the elevator. Once Anna had been rolled inside and the elevator door closed, Howard turned around, fell to his knees, put his hands on his face and began crying. But it was Moe, rather than Howard, who took the ride in the ambulance with Anna to the hospital. And it was Moe, about a half an hour later in the emergency room of Memorial Regional Hospital, who gave doctors the nod to stop their resuscitation efforts.

At 2:49 p.m. Anna Nicole Smith was pronounced dead. Since the hospital chaplain wasn't available, Moe leaned down and whispered a prayer over the body of the former Playboy Playmate he had been in charge of guarding. He gave Anna her last rites and told her to go be with her son.

Howard eventually went to the hospital, but not at his request. An eyewitness says after thirty minutes to an hour of him being in the room and talking to detectives, the hospital called and asked for Howard's presence. Another person on scene told me, "He was in no rush to go."

● ● ●

Howard K. Stern had been quite busy. He began talking to his media contacts right away, which surprised several people around him. The timing of this detail has never been made public before. *Entertainment Tonight*, which had previously made exclusive "deals" with the couple, was already en route to Hollywood, Florida, and was confirmed for a block of rooms at the Hard Rock that Howard personally called to reserve before 4 p.m. Given that Anna had just been pronounced dead at 2:49 p.m., it was shocking to many of those present that Howard could even think of any media at that moment, much less make an exclusive deal so soon after her death pronouncement. But he did. "Right away," said an eyewitness, "Howard was ready to make his next deal. It showed us that to Howard it was all about money."

CHAPTER 2

Next of Kin

"I JUST WANT HER TO BE WITH DANIEL," HOWARD K. STERN cried to *Entertainment Tonight* cameras on his flight from Florida to the Bahamas on *Entertainment Tonight*'s private plane. Even though Howard testified under oath during the Florida court hearing over Anna's burial that he only received the free flight, he was reportedly paid one million dollars to allow the entertainment news magazine to exclusively tape him and tag along as he went back to the Bahamas to secure Anna's five-month-old baby, Dannielynn—the baby he was claiming to be the father of.

Anna would, as Howard hoped, soon be with her beloved son Daniel, side by side in burial plots purchased in the Bahamas in the fall. Stern himself testified that he signed the check for the cemetery property, four family plots, one for each of them for the future, precipitated by her twenty-year-old son's death five months prior to Anna's. Daniel died under similar sudden and mysterious circumstances while visiting Howard, his mother, and newborn sister in a Bahamian hospital.

Drug infused death seems to run in the family.

• • •

The summer before his death, Daniel Wayne Smith was taking classes at Los Angeles Valley College—getting an "A" in his philosophy class. He had gotten his driver's license, and was living with Ray Martino, one of Anna's long-time friends and the director of *To the Limit* and *Anna Nicole Smith: Exposed*, a video collection of Anna's "most delicious fantasies . . . complete with exotic French maids, lusty limo drivers, and bubble baths." Anna didn't worry about Daniel finding out about or being exposed to her naughty side. She'd raised Daniel to be around adults, unabashedly exposing him to her life. He knew everything about her: from her stripper past to her Howard present.

And, according to private investigator Jack Harding, it was the overbearing presence of Howard that inspired the young man to call the seasoned investigator for a meeting. Daniel had met the seventy-four-year-old Jack Harding through Ray Martino in the summer of 2006, shortly before Daniel died. He was having a hard time with his mother's recent decision to move to the Bahamas, thousands of miles away from him. In fact, he ended up in the hospital on two occasions during that summer—shortly before Anna moved and on July 17, the day before she arrived in the Bahamas to establish permanent residency. He complained of stomach cramps and back pain. Doctors thought he was depressed and incredibly stressed.

Ray Martino treated Daniel like a son and, trying to help him look toward the future, introduced him to Jack Harding because Daniel said he was interested in the military. Harding, a friend of Ray's, had served in the military years ago and the two of them struck up a conversation about what that was like.

Daniel kept the private investigator's business card and called him in August, about a month after the two had initially met. He told the private investigator that he "wanted to meet about business this time." They met early the next night at Paty's Restaurant on Riverside Drive in Toluca Lake.

Daniel, tall and slender, was wearing a shirt over his t-shirt, as well as jeans and a baseball cap. They didn't eat, but during their hour and a half chat over coffee and tea, Daniel kept looking out the window, around the restaurant, and admitted he was very worried someone was following him. He told Harding that he didn't want anyone to know that he was meeting with him, not even Ray with whom he was staying.

He told Harding about a dream he had had the night before in which he saw his mom in a coffin. "She was looking grey," Daniel said, his eyes welling with tears. "He was clearly upset," Harding told me. "He was so emotional and disturbed by this dream. I could not dismiss it."

He told Harding he wanted him to investigate what Howard K. Stern was doing to his mom and people around her. Daniel said, "Every time I call the Bahamas' house, Howard hangs up on me." He also felt Howard had ordered others on Anna's staff to do the same, preventing Daniel from talking to her. "Howard also keeps feeding my mom drugs," he continued, "mind-bending drugs. He has total control over her like a, like a . . ."

"Svengali?" Harding asked.

"Yeah," Daniel said. "That's it! He's a Svengali. Howard does not want me around because I want to get my mom off the drugs and away from him . . . to save her." He explained

30

that ever since Howard had come into their lives, he had purposely kept his mother "out of it all the time." Harding said Ray Martino had told him before that Anna had cleaned up for a while, but had gone "off the deep end with drugs" when she hooked up with Howard.

Daniel also told the private investigator that Howard was having people "lay his mom"—pimping her for sex. Daniel didn't elaborate further to Harding. However, Jackie Hatten, Daniel's godmother, told me Daniel confided in her that "he'd seen Howard give his mom uppers and downers and then guys would come to the house, talk to Howard and go in his mom's bedroom and close the door." According to Jackie, Daniel called it the "Millionaire's Club," a reference to an episode on Anna's E! Entertainment Television reality show, in which she had gone out on arranged dates with super wealthy men. Unlike the show, however, Daniel told Jackie that the men he saw, at least fifty of them in a year, would go into his mom's bedroom for hours. Then, from his vantage point hiding behind the door in his bedroom, he'd see the guys coming out adjusting their clothes and discretely palming Howard money on the way out the door. Daniel said he'd then see his mom being "all drugged out and groggy" in her bedroom.

"Daniel definitely didn't want to say anything bad about his mom," Harding said. "He was very protective and loved his mom." And, according to Jackie and other friends of Anna's, though her sexual proclivities were wild and well known, she was adamantly against prostitution. Jackie said she and Daniel firmly believed Anna had no idea Howard was getting paid on the side. "When Anna was not sober, she was easy to take advantage of. My friend Anna was Howard Stern's cash cow. Howard was taking advantage of Anna in every way, up until, and including, her death."

Daniel also told Jack Harding that he saw Howard give his mom drugs. "He gave everyone drugs," he told the P.I., "including me." He added that he had gotten himself off the drugs and was now clean. Harding noted that Daniel's eyes were clear that night. He was absolutely coherent, he did not slur his words or appear to be on drugs in any way.

Daniel told Harding that the reason he wanted to go join the military was that he could learn to be a strong fighter, to "be a man and take my mom away from Howard." Then, Daniel's voice turned low, like he was scared someone was listening. "I am deathly afraid of him and very scared for my mother. Howard hates me and keeps me away from her. That's how he treats all my mom's friends. He's made her a prisoner. I want to get my mom out of there."

Daniel said he wanted Harding to gather all this information against Howard in case Howard came after him physically and so Daniel could use the evidence versus Howard in a court of law. He said he feared what Howard would do to him, and knew that Howard did not like him because he had stood up to him a few times. "It's clear Howard wants me out of the picture," Daniel said. "So he can have complete control of my mom and all the money coming into her hands." In a will that was drafted in 2001, Daniel was listed as the sole heir to Anna's estate, which eventually could reach into the hundreds of millions of dollars if she was victorious in her court battles with the estate of her late billionaire husband, J. Howard Marshall.

Jack Harding told Daniel he'd take his case, but he would have to go to the Bahamas to investigate. He then told Daniel about his rates. "I normally charge three hundred dollars an hour," he said. "But it would be much more if I have to travel to a place like the Bahamas. You'd have to pay the hourly rate, plus travel, hotel, rental car, and food." He'd have to spend thousands of dollars because he would probably have to be in the Bahamas for several days up to several weeks to question and do surveillance on people, especially on Howard K. Stern.

The costs, of course, were well beyond what Daniel had imagined. "I don't have any money now," Daniel confessed, "since I am not getting any money coming in, but I am hoping to get some soon and maybe we can start now." He asked Harding if he'd work immediately and get paid later, but Harding explained that he's been in the business for over thirty years and for a project like this he'd need some money up front.

Daniel was very upset, but understood.

"So, the last time I saw Daniel," Harding remembered, "was when he walked out the door of the restaurant."

A month later, Daniel would be dead. Bahamian Police would find Jack Harding's business card in Daniel's pocket, in the clothes he was wearing when he took his last breath.

Saturday, September 9, 2006

For most of his life, Daniel Smith was at his mother's side when she needed him. So at 10:25 p.m. on September 9, 2006, two days after she had given birth to his sister, Daniel arrived in Nassau on American Eagle flight 5005.

Anna had called and told him, "You have a baby sister!" and asked him to come down. Daniel hadn't been feeling well the day he was supposed to fly from Los Angeles to the Bahamas. He told Ray Martino he had a stomachache. But he wanted to see his mother. It had been months since he'd seen her—one of the longest periods of times they had spent apart—and they had always had a very close relationship.

Anna's brother, Donnie Hogan, said Anna adored Daniel, and had big hopes for her son. "She told me her best success was Daniel," Donnie said. "She was always holding and hugging him. Nothing was more important to her than Daniel.

"I remember when Daniel was six or seven and we were at her ranch in Tomball [Texas]. Daniel was leaning on a fence, missing his front teeth, and told everyone, 'I'll be a big actor one day,' and Anna said, 'Whatever he'll be, he's going to be a star.'"

Daniel loved to laugh and to make people laugh. When Daniel was around eight years old, Donnie, Daniel, and Anna were in a car, stopped at a light. There was a homeless man with signs sitting on the corner, and Daniel rolled down the window and asked, "Pardon me, but do you have any Grey Poupon?" mimicking a popular commercial on at the time. They all laughed, but Anna quickly told him that those men were less fortunate than he was and that it was not the right thing to do.

Anna's good friend, Jackie Hatten, used to pick Daniel up from school when he was younger. She says Daniel rarely cursed and always respected his mom, doing whatever she asked, even the laundry. Daniel was intelligent, sweet, and, like many young men, loved video games like Mortal Combat and movies, especially Ben Stiller's *Zoolander*, about a dimwitted male model whose "spiky black hair" and patented model pose, "Blue Steel," made him the envy of the fashion world.

Around the time of Anna's move to the Bahamas, stress and depression led to Daniel losing weight—twenty to thirty pounds—and breaking up with a woman he was dating. On July 17, the day before Anna flew to the Bahamas from South Carolina, Daniel was shaking and his heart was racing. He was depressed to the point of breakdown. Ray Martino took him to St. Joseph's Medical Center in Burbank and Daniel was admitted. He spent four days undergoing a battery of tests, including tests for drugs. Doctors found nothing remarkable.

Daniel told a close family friend that he was depressed and very worried about his mom. Soon after he left the hospital, one of his mother's many doctors, Sandeep Kapoor—the man who wrote her prescriptions for methadone—wrote Daniel a prescription for Lexapro, one of the two antidepressants found in his system when he died. These two drugs were in lethal combination with another drug found in his system . . . methadone, a prescription of which his mother had received less than a month before.

• • •

Jackie Hatten spoke to Daniel a couple of months before he died. According to Jackie, Daniel was scared of Howard and all the drugs he kept giving to Anna. He asked Jackie if she would go to the Bahamas with him, saying he was scared to be alone with Howard there. Jackie told him that Howard didn't like her very much and would probably be really mad if she came along. Still, she warned him not to go alone.

Daniel was under intense stress and told her he wanted to go down to the Bahamas to "save" his mother. He told Jackie, as he would later also tell private investigator Jack Harding, that Howard wouldn't let him talk to his mother and that Howard had cut off communications between them.

But Howard claimed communications were just fine. He painted the relationship with Daniel much rosier than Daniel had described it to others. "Daniel to me was a great friend, a brother," Howard K. Stern would tell Larry King on September 26, just two weeks after Daniel's death. "I loved Daniel . . . part of me just wishes I would wake up and this whole thing has been an elaborate nightmare."

Perhaps it was the other part of him that caused Daniel so much angst.

• • •

Though Howard suggested during that TV interview that Daniel intended to move to the Bahamas "to stay with his mom and go to school here," even Howard's own friends told me that Daniel never planned to stay there. His plan was to visit for a short while, one to three weeks maximum. Daniel didn't like the Bahamas because he couldn't stand the heat.

The night before he left, while Ray Martino helped him pack, Daniel asked Ray if he'd go with him, but Ray said he couldn't because of work. Daniel admitted that he was very nervous to go. Ray thought it was just because Daniel didn't like to fly.

The morning of his flight Ray took him to the Burbank Airport and bought him French toast for breakfast. Before he boarded the flight—from Burbank to Fort Worth, then to Miami for a quick flight to the Bahamas—Jack Harding says Ray told him he gave Daniel "a couple of Valiums" for his nerves.

"Don't leave me down there," Daniel said.

"I won't," Ray promised.

Daniel boarded the plane.

• • •

At 10:30 p.m. Howard picked Daniel up in Nassau and drove him to Doctor's Hospital where two days prior his mother had had a C-section delivery. Around 11 p.m. they arrived at the hospital—a modern facility with 72 beds on Collins Avenue in

Nassau—and Daniel rushed into room 201 and gave his mother a big hug. Anna introduced Daniel to the baby and handed the little bundle to him, saying to the as-yet-unnamed baby, "Here's your brother, Daniel."

"Look at her, Momma," he said, his eyes filled with excitement. "She's looking at me!" Daniel was in great spirits. He played with the baby's fingers and held her like she was his own. He was happy, lively, and completely alert.

Ben Thompson, a former boyfriend of Anna's and the man who owned the Horizons house where she was living, was in the room visiting Anna and her newborn when Daniel got there. He told me that Daniel was "thrilled to death" to be with Anna and to meet his little sister.

Howard pulled out his camera and took pictures as Daniel and Anna reunited and as Daniel proudly rocked his new baby sister in his arms. "It was great," Howard later said. "It was like one of the best nights that I've ever remembered. I mean Anna was so content. She had her son and her new baby girl, and I was there and it was great."

Sunday, September 10

A little after midnight, Ben Thompson left the room so that Anna and Daniel could spend some quality time with each other, and Ben could get some sleep. Shortly after he left, Anna, Daniel, and Howard decided they were hungry. In the Bahamas there isn't much open late at night, so Howard made a food run to a 24-hour mini-mart inside a nearby Esso gas station. He bought chips, soft drinks, and fried chicken strips, Anna and Daniel's favorite. (Ironic, considering Anna had gotten pregnant with Daniel when she was seventeen-years-old and working as a waitress at Jim's Krispy Fried Chicken in Mexia, Texas.)

When Howard returned with the food, they sat around Anna's bed and ate, a late-night celebratory party. There were two hospital beds and a large armchair in her room, and Anna was in the bed closest to the window. The other bed Howard offered to Daniel, but Daniel said he wasn't really that tired and said Howard could take it. The seemingly healthy twenty-year-old was going to stay up and watch some television. Daniel settled into the armchair; Howard took the other bed.

Since Anna had a C-section just two days before, she was still quite weak and needed help getting to the bathroom, and, according to Howard, Daniel helped her to the bathroom "many times throughout the night."

"At one point Daniel said to me, 'how come I'm so tired?'" Howard recounted on *Larry King Live*. "And, in hindsight, I wish that I had seen that as some sort of a signal and seen that something wasn't right."

Several investigators have indicated to me that the statement was peculiar. Why would Howard have seen a young man being tired in the middle of the night after a day's travel from the opposite side of the continent as "a signal?" Why would that have indicated "something wasn't right?"

"Unless," as one investigator put it, "Howard knew that Daniel had taken something. Or, more to the point, been given something."

According to Doctor's Hospital records, a nurse making her rounds noted that at 6:20 a.m. Daniel was attending to his mother's comfort. Subsequently, during the hourly rounds, he was observed to be asleep on multiple nurse visits.

Shortly after 9:30 a.m., Anna tried to wake Daniel who had moved into the bed with her. Though he appeared sound asleep, he was lifeless. "Howard!" she yelled. "Howard! Daniel's not breathing." Howard jumped out of bed and went to her bedside.

"I checked Daniel's neck, and I didn't feel anything," he said. "We called the nurses and said it was an emergency."

At 9:38 a.m., according to hospital records, the nurse was called to room 201, following which physicians on the floor were immediately summoned and straight away initiated CPR. A code blue was called and a team rushed from the emergency room. For twenty-two minutes, resuscitative efforts using Advanced Life Support Protocol continued on the lifeless body of Daniel, without response.

Though they tried to get Anna to leave the room, she refused. She was hysterical. At some point early in the desperate chaos, Howard called Ben Thompson at the Horizons house and told him, "You need to get to the hospital as quick as you can. It's not good." He also found time to call Ray Martino in California, waking him up, and pleading with him to come to the Bahamas right away.

Anna moved to the foot of the bed where she grabbed Daniel's leg and kept hugging it. Anna and Daniel often spoke about the Catholic Church, and the Playboy Playmate was known to pray to Mary every day. As doctors tried their last futile efforts, Anna was screaming and praying to Jesus and she was telling Jesus to take her and not take Daniel. It was an awful scene.

At 10:05 a.m. Daniel Wayne Smith was pronounced dead.

After the hospital gave up resuscitation efforts, Anna refused to. She screamed "No, no!" and continued trying to revive her dead son.

"There was an airbag that they were putting air in," Howard later told Larry King. "And she had me doing that and she was

39

pumping on his chest. And I just, you know, I don't know. I'm not a doctor."

Anna just didn't want to believe that he had died. She wanted to keep going. She insisted they keep trying to bring Daniel back to life. She was screaming so loudly, her desperate cries could be heard down the halls of the hospital.

When Ben Thompson arrived at the hospital around 10:30 a.m., about an hour after the emergency call came from the room, security was already clamped down. Ben came through the back entrance and when he got off the elevator, a hospital employee told him Daniel was dead. Though hospital security was checking everyone who was coming or going, the hospital room, a potential crime scene, seemed to be unobserved.

When Ben went into the hospital room, Daniel was in the bed and Anna was in bed with him. There was barely six inches on the bed for her to place her body and Ben was worried because she just had a C-section. She was holding him and hugging him, screaming out his nickname, "Pumpkin! Pumpkin!" She was hysterical.

"The doctors advised us that we should probably check her out of the hospital because the media was going to be coming," Howard said. "And it was going to . . . make the situation even worse." Bahamian law requires autopsies to be performed on any unexplained death, but she refused to leave her son. Before Daniel's body was transferred to the Rand Lab, Anna had to be sedated.

But before that, Howard grabbed his camera and said, "Let me get a picture." And he started taking photos of Anna Nicole Smith, lying in a hospital bed cradling her dead son.

The last set of snapshots was not included in the group of photos capturing Daniel's last hours that was sold to *In Touch* magazine for a reported $600,000 and to *Entertainment Tonight* for an undisclosed sum. When Howard listed the pictures with a photo service, they were photos of Daniel's arrival, not of his departure.

"When we heard that the photos were available," *In Touch* magazine news editor Linda Massarella told CBS's *The Early Show*, "my immediate reaction was we have to get them. I want to see that. Everybody is going to want to see that."

Dan Wakeford, the magazine's executive editor, said he secured the photos from Getty Images, but declined to identify the photographer.

"It's a loving photo just after she gave birth, with Daniel," Massarella said. "It's the family snapshot, it's the last family snapshot."

Not quite. The very last photographs were actually held back, but I have personally seen one of these pictures and it is quite disturbing.

It shows a crying Anna Nicole Smith lying on her right side in her hospital bed. Rather than holding her precious three-day-old daughter, she is instead cradling the dead body of her beloved twenty-year-old son. Her right arm, crooked beneath Daniel's head, is still bearing a bracelet adapted with an intravenous tube; her left arm, wearing a red hospital wristband, caresses Daniel's cheek. His face is as stark white as the hospital blanket pulled up about his neck, and a breathing tube protrudes from his mouth. His eyes are partially open.

The one I saw is a painfully gruesome photo. How anyone could have taken it during a mother's darkest hour is a question that all who've seen it have asked.

CHAPTER 3

Life After Death

WITHIN HOURS OF DANIEL'S DEATH, HOWARD OVERHEARD Anna tell Ben Thompson, "I probably need to call my momma."

"Let's wait to call her later," Howard said.

Virgie Arthur, Anna's mother, like so many other people in Anna's life, had found herself shut out. And Virgie, like so many other people in Anna's life, blamed it on Howard. "He kept all of us from her, not just me," Virgie would tell me shortly after Anna's death. "He kept her whole family away from her. He kept her to himself. People that loved her tried to help her. Those that didn't love her, lived with her and lived off her."

By the time Anna did finally call her mother's house in Texas several days later, Virgie had already learned from TV news that her grandson was dead. Anna's speech was slurred and Virgie could tell that her daughter was under the influence of drugs. "She was mumbling like a drunk does," Virgie said. "All I got out of it was 'Danny's dead. Momma he's gone, he's gone . . . but he's coming back. He's coming back.' And then it sounded. . . . It was like she was in the middle of a sentence and the phone went click. And that's all I got to hear from her."

It would be the last time Virgie Arthur personally heard from her daughter.

Sunday, September 10, early afternoon

From the moments immediately following Daniel's death, until the day Anna died, she was often in a drug haze, a blurry void somewhere between conscious and unconscious.

The normally joyous occasion of taking a newborn baby home from the hospital was filled with overwhelming sadness for Anna Nicole Smith, even though she had long hoped for a little girl. Anna's new friends, Immigration Minister Shane Gibson and Theresa Laramore, came to take the three-day-old unnamed baby of the as yet unnamed father, out of the chaos of room 201 after Daniel's death. Anna Nicole's new baby was whisked away quickly out the back door of the hospital to avoid attention. Anna Nicole stayed behind, clinging to the body of Daniel.

It is a mother's worst nightmare—the birth of one child, the death of another. According to eyewitnesses, it was a terribly emotional, pitiful scene—having her son die in her hospital bed in a foreign country where she had just given birth, and then refusing to let them take his body to the morgue. Anna Nicole was uncontrollable, delirious, and had to be sedated before she would finally let go of Daniel's body.

When Anna's grasp of reality and on her child had lessened, Daniel's body was taken out of her bed to the morgue for the mandatory autopsy. After Howard gave police his recollection of what had happened since Daniel's arrival, he, Ben, and several others loaded everything into Ben's rented van, and a heavily tranquilized, sobbing Anna was helped to the car. Rather than sealing the room and its contents, police weren't acting like the hospital room was a crime scene, so Howard and Anna were free to remove all their belongings— Anna's clothes, flowers sent to the hospital for her newborn, even Daniel's suitcase and some of Daniel's clothes that medical personnel had stripped from his body in the fruitless attempts to save his life.

They were also able to remove what numerous friends have described as Howard's "goodie bag." Howard typically carried either a brown Coach bag or a black duffle bag. It was a repository for an assortment of drugs, which, according to employees, friends, and court testimony, he doled out to Anna on an "as-he-thought-she-needed" basis.

"He was the pharmacist and that was the drugstore," Ben Thompson said. So much so that friends would later find it ironic when Larry King asked Howard K. Stern if Lexapro was an antidepressant, and Howard answered, "I'm not too familiar with how medications work but, yes, it's an anti–depressant."

Anna's friend Jackie Hatten told me she's witnessed Howard giving Anna a medley of drugs: "Vicodin, Valium, morphine, Demerol, you name it, he had it."

As they were leaving the hospital, Howard asked Ben to watch over the duffle bag and the camera bag, after he had taken a number of photos of Daniel. "I don't understand why the Bahamian Police didn't lock down that hospital room," Ben said. But they didn't. The bags were free to go.

"Don't let them out of your sight," Howard said, pointing to the camera bag. "Anna's life is in that bag."

As they left the hospital that tragic September day, two pills weren't in Howard's "goodie bag"—the two that were found in the bed where Howard had slept. Those two pills were now in a plastic bag and being held by the Bahamian police as possible evidence.

That morning when Nadine Carey, the nurse on duty at 9:38 a.m., heard "Code Blue" she hurried to room 201 and found the medical team rushing around the bed where Daniel Smith lay lifeless. The medical equipment, life-saving apparatus, and numerous people, including a wailing Anna Nicole, were crowding the room. In order to free up space, Carey pulled the bed nearest the door out and into the hall in order to give doctors better access to try and work their miracles on Daniel's breathless body. When she did, she noticed two white tablets on top of the sheets, one smaller than the other. Following protocol, she gave them to the doctor on duty, the doctor gave them to his supervisor, and then the two pills were passed on to the Bahamian police constable, who put them in a plastic bag and sent them away for testing.

When Howard recounted the story of that awful morning two weeks later on *Larry King Live*, he pointedly made mention that Daniel had also spent time in that bed. "At first I was going to sleep on the floor in between the two beds," he explained, "and Daniel was in the bed closest to the door. And, Daniel at some point said to me that, you know, he wasn't really that tired, so why didn't I just take the bed and he was going to sit up and watch TV."

But according to at least three nurses on duty, Daniel was never in that bed. "Only the man was in the bed," they each said. Contrary to Howard's story, the nurses said in their initial statements to police that it was Howard and only Howard who had been in that other hospital bed as each made their rounds that night and early morning. Daniel had been in the chair, then at 5:30 a.m. he had moved into the same bed with his mother. None of the nurses saw Daniel in the bed nearest the door.

The two pills found in the bed where the nurses saw Howard sleeping were determined to be methadone, a synthetic narcotic used to treat opiate addicts, and Carisoprodol, a muscle relaxant. Anna Nicole had prescriptions for both medications. In fact, Dr. Sandeep Kapoor, Anna's Los Angeles based doctor, wrote a prescription for methadone on August 25, 2006, just thirteen days before she gave birth. The prescription, RX#2846735, was written for Michelle Chase, one of Anna Nicole's favorite aliases. Key Pharmacy in the San Fernando Valley had filled the prescription, which was sent to "Vicky Marshall" (sic) at a Harbour Bay Shopping Plaza post office box on East Bay Street in Nassau, Bahamas. Under California law, it's illegal to prescribe a controlled substance to a false name.

Bahamian Police did find something interesting on Daniel's body that wasn't cleared and packed into Ben Thompson's rented van. They'd found a business card in one of Daniel's pockets. The business card was that of Jack Harding, the private investigator Daniel had met with the month before he died. The man whom Daniel had told how deathly afraid he was of Howard K. Stern. Jack Harding told me, "When I heard that Daniel died, I was shocked but not surprised that Stern could be there and be involved somehow."

A few weeks after Daniel's death, California private eye Jack Harding got a call from a detective at the Burbank Police Department asking if he had been in the Bahamas investigating for Daniel Smith, and if so, informing him that he was in violation of Bahamian law. Forty-five minutes later the officer, along with four Bahamian police officers and an "official looking" man in a light colored suit showed up at Jack Harding's house and questioned him for an hour in his living room. Harding told me that they asked him, "Why did the boy call you?" and "Why did he have your card?"

The Drug Enforcement Agency and the California Medical Association have also called asking him about Howard and drugs.

But the Bahamian police weren't the only surprise visitors the private eye had. In April of 2007, two months after Anna's death, at 8:45 p.m., Jack Harding's three dogs went bolting through his backyard, barking madly. He went to see what the commotion was and caught a man trying to sneak over his fence.

"Are you Jack Harding?" the man asked, dogs growling at his feet.

"Yep," Harding answered.

"Well, I'm John Nazarian, and I'm retained by Howard K. Stern."

He handed Harding his business card: "John Nazarian of Nazarian and Associates, Investigations and Securities." Harding said the card had an interesting e-mail address on it: "willspy4money@aol.com."

In June of 2006, the *Los Angeles Times* ran a front-page piece on John Nazarian, a fifty-five-year-old Hollywood gumshoe in the Sam Spade tradition. He, like many of the 2,100 licensed private eyes in Los Angeles County, are the hired guns the celebrities call when they need their problems to disappear. Nazarian, who claims to get $10,000 to $20,000 retainers and

$400 an hour, has worked for a number of celebrity clients, including Peggy Lee (whom he protected from paparazzi), Dean Martin, and the television show *Extra*, which sent him to Mexico to hunt for Olivia Newton-John's boyfriend, who had disappeared after a fishing trip.

Nazarian is also the only investigator used by the "dean of L.A. divorce lawyers," Sorrell Trope. Trope and Trope is the law firm where Ron Rale works. Ron Rale is the man who has been vigorously defending Howard K. Stern even though he says he's not Howard's attorney. He says he merely oversees the interests of Anna. But Ron Rale is said to be the one who introduced Howard K. Stern to Anna and is also listed, along with Howard, as the secondary executor of her will.

"Lots of people are trying to be private investigators or security experts," John Nazarian says on his website, "but there is only one proven LEGEND." Certainly, Nazarian's interesting tactics have gained him a notorious reputation. Lynn Soodik, an attorney specializing in family law, told the *Los Angeles Times* that Nazarian definitely tried to intimidate her during a case against one of Nazarian's clients. He sent a greeting card to her at home. "On the surface, it was not threatening," she said, "but you knew he was saying, 'I know where you live.'"

Nazarian told the paper he also went through her trash, just to unnerve her. "Not that we break the law," he said, "but a private eye, by the mere fact of what we do, it's not like we're a bunch of choirboys. We're not."

Incidentally, neighbors would later tell Harding that they saw a man in the neighborhood fitting Nazarian's description taking pictures of Harding's house.

A former cop, Nazarian has a team of experts who work with him—a handwriting analyst, a forensic accountant, a lab technician, and technology whizzes—but it is perhaps his menacing looks and reputation that often goes the farthest to getting the job done. He looks like a professional wrestler, shaving his head like Kojak and shaping his black dyed goatee into an interesting wing-like spread across his jaw. His typical attire includes a hat, oversize designer shades, and lots of "bling." He owns a cream-colored Bentley and a Rolls Royce and wears two chunky trademark rings of gold and platinum that look like two squashed golf balls sitting atop his knuckles.

"I'm looking for a guy who's 75," Nazarian told fellow P.I. Jack Harding as they stood in Harding's backyard shortly after Anna's death. Seventy-four-year-old Jack Harding knew the game being played. He was being intimidated. He was being not so subtly told to keep his mouth shut about what he knows. Nazarian then made comments such as "Hey, this is a good area you live in" and "Your house is worth a lot. You need to protect that place."

"He was definitely threatening me and letting me know he's been doing research on me," Jack Harding told me. "It was clear that Howard K. Stern had sent his goon over to intimidate me."

Sunday, September 10, afternoon into evening

As Daniel's body went to the morgue to await its mandatory autopsy, his mother was taken back to Horizons, the Bahamian home her former boyfriend Ben Thompson had signed over to her so that she could meet the Bahamian residency requirements.

On almost one acre, the gated estate on Eastern Road in New Providence is lushly landscaped and has panoramic water views. The all-white, neo-Mediterranean style house is protected like a fortress behind locked gates and privacy bushes. Verandas and terraces overlook pristine gardens, a tennis court, and a gothic looking pool with Grecian statues.

But besides the work of gardeners and handymen, activity on the outside of the house for Anna Nicole Smith was rare. It was inside the three-bedroom, three-bath house where all the drama occurred. She was sequestered inside the waterfront mansion, like an aging beauty hiding from the flash of cameras, or worse. She was a depressed new mother, who'd just lost her beloved other child, and was infused with mind-numbing drugs.

An employee who started working for them as soon as she and Howard moved to the house and stayed on for seven months up until her death, earned Anna's trust and confidence. He became her confidante. Later, he told me that "Howard never treated her right," and that what went on inside the house, both before and after Daniel's death, was "terrible and rocky." He said, "He'd cuss at her. I saw him push her down on the bed a couple of times. I asked her about it and she said, 'don't worry with it. He'll get over it.' She didn't want no hard feelings from me toward Howard, so she told me just to leave it at that."

"He pushed her on the bed once and said, 'Get your fat, fucking ass away from me.' I walked in and he stopped. She just started crying. She told me everything would be okay . . . . I saw a lot. I know a lot."

"Why did she tolerate the abuse?" I asked.

"He had something on her that she couldn't bring to the public," he said. "She was afraid of him because he had something on her."

• • •

When they got back to the Horizons house the day Daniel died, Ben and Anna went to Howard's bedroom, while Gaither Thompson, Ben's son, and Ford Shelley, Ben's son-in-law, went to Anna's bedroom where Howard had started rifling through all of Daniel's things. Howard and Anna had separate bedrooms, approximately one hundred feet apart. While Ben comforted Anna, Ford says Howard was aggressively searching through Daniel's jeans, his shoes, his t-shirt, and baseball cap, which were all laid out on the bed in Anna's room.

Both Gaither and Ford saw two pills fall out of Daniel's front pocket. "They were two white tablets," Ford Shelley said, "odd shaped. I'm not sure what they were."

Howard took the pills, went into the bathroom and closed the door. Suspicious of what Howard was doing, Ford walked over to the bathroom door and heard the toilet flush. When he came out of the bathroom, Ford Shelley says Howard proclaimed, "I took care of the problem."

"Why are you doing this?" Ford asked. "I wouldn't have done that if I were you."

After a long pause, Howard said, "Well, I did."

Ford believes Howard was protecting Daniel and Anna, but told me, "Jesus Christ! I can't believe he'd destroy evidence like that." Ford also told me, "I believe Howard was doing what Anna told him to do. I believe Anna told him to make sure anything suspicious was gone. No matter how drunken and out of it Anna was, she was still aware and knew she could not have drug evidence tied to Daniel."

It should not go unnoted that Anna had been heavily sedated since the hospital—hallucinating and saying she wanted Daniel to come watch a movie with her. Anna would later say she had no memory of the morning her son suddenly and mysteriously died.

Ford Shelley never spoke to Howard about those two pills again.

Monday, September 11

Bahamian coroner Linda Virgill called to ask Anna to come identify the body of her son, and Anna, overwrought with sadness and heavily medicated, signed a paper allowing Howard to make the positive identification. Howard K. Stern and Ford Shelley went to the morgue and identified the body as being Daniel Wayne Smith, the twenty-year-old son of the woman known as Anna Nicole Smith.

At the morgue Linda Virgill told Howard that she wanted to come to the house and ask Anna questions about her son's death. Howard told her Anna wasn't up to visitors, that it would be better if she could come at a later time. Linda Virgill said no, she was going to the house now. Howard and Ford said they were hungry and wanted to stop and grab a bite to eat. Linda Virgill wasn't hungry and wanted no delays. There was no stopping. She was going to the house immediately.

On the drive back to the house Howard and Ford Shelley were in a separate vehicle from Virgill. According to Shelley, Howard called and told someone on the other end of the phone, "Go put the pills away now!" He explained the coroner was on the way, and added, "Put the pills in the bag under the bed or in the bed in the master bedroom."

The master bedroom was Anna's bedroom.

"What are you doing?" Ford asked. "Maybe Daniel took something that would've killed him."

For the rest of the drive, Howard was silent. "He clearly

wanted to hide those pills before the coroner got there and started snooping around," Ford said.

When they arrived at the house, Linda Virgill asked a lot of questions about drugs, prescriptions, and that night in the hospital. She also looked around the minimally decorated house, taking in the home environment of the Bahamas' newest celebrity resident. Ford Shelley says Howard repeatedly told Linda Virgill, as he would also tell other Bahamian authorities, that there were no drugs present and no drug history for Daniel. "There is no way any drugs could've played a role," Howard said.

Ford says he was shocked by Howard's clear lie. They knew Howard had taken those pills out of Daniel's pocket before he made those statements to the coroner and also had all the pills in the house as well as the "goodie bag" put away. "He had already tampered with evidence," Ford said.

That night, the air conditioning in Anna's bedroom didn't work, and when Ford, his wife, and Howard lifted the mattress to move it into another room to sleep on, his "goodie bag" fell from between Anna's mattress where it had been hidden and onto the floor. Howard picked it up, gave it to Ford's wife and instructed her to "put it in a safe, concealed place."

In talking with Ford Shelley and Ben Thompson about Linda Virgill's last minute visit that day, Howard announced, "We need to get her removed. She's going to be a problem."

Wednesday, September 13

Two days later, Her Majesty's coroner Linda P. Virgill announced the death of Daniel Wayne Smith was "suspicious" and scheduled a formal inquiry, an "inquest," which could lead to criminal charges. Bradley Neely, chief inspector of the coroner's office, was quick to explain to the Associated Press, "Whenever there is a suspicious death we would have an inquest to determine how the person died."

Virgill went further, saying authorities believe they knew what killed Daniel, but said that the autopsy and toxicology reports would not be released until the inquest. "It would not be fair to the Bahamian public simply because we need to take our jurors from that pool and you do not wish to contaminate them," she told reporters. She did, however, say that there was no sign of physical injury and confirmed rather ominously that "there was definitely a third person in the room at the time of death and I do know who that person is."

The inquest was scheduled for the week of October 23. If jurors at the inquest were to decide that a crime took place, the case would then be sent to the attorney general's office.

Reginald Ferguson, the assistant commissioner of the Royal Bahamian Police Force, told the press that no drug paraphernalia or traces of illegal drugs were found on Daniel Smith, in the hospital room, or near the room.

He didn't mention the two pills that nurse Nadine Carey found in the bed of the "third person" in the room, the bed where Howard K. Stern had slept.

Thursday, September 14

The following day in a continued volley, Michael Scott, the Bahamian attorney representing Anna, delivered a prepared statement. "The devastation and grief over Daniel's sudden death, coupled with the sedation, has been so extreme that

Anna Nicole experienced memory loss of the event." He went on to say that "Anna Nicole was so distraught at the loss of Daniel that she refused to leave his side and it was necessary to sedate her in order to check her out of the hospital." Later, he said, Anna had to be reminded that Daniel had passed away.

In concluding his statement, Michael Scott said he wanted to clear up the mystery of the third person in the room. It wasn't a mystery or even unusual. The third person in the room was "another one of Anna Nicole Smith's attorneys," a man named Howard K. Stern.

Sunday, September 17

Expert examiner Dr. Cyril Wecht, who has performed approximately 14,000 autopsies and has supervised, reviewed or been consulted on approximately 30,000 additional postmortem examinations, was brought to the Bahamas by Callender and Company, the Bahamian law firm of Michael Scott, to perform a second autopsy "on behalf of the family." Dr. Wecht, a frequent cable news guest, has been utilized in many high profile cases including the 1969 drowning death of Kennedy campaign worker Mary Jo Kopechne, the murder case of American heiress Sunny von Bulow, and the strange suicide of Whitewater figure Vincent Foster. Now, after spending three hours in a chilly morgue on a hot Sunday afternoon in the Bahamas, Dr. Cyril Wecht has added Daniel Wayne Smith to the list.

According to Dr. Wecht, he found no scratches or marks on Daniel's body, and blood tests ruled out the presence of alcohol and other drugs including cocaine, opiates and amphetamines. The procedure he performed detailed Daniel's death as an accidental lethal combination of two anti-depressants—Zoloft and Lexapro—and methadone. Though methadone is supposed to be carefully administered by a doctor and has typically not been thought of as a "street drug," recreational use of the drug has become a problem. According to Wecht, Daniel had no known addiction to morphine or heroin. Methadone is commonly used to wean people off of those drugs.

Since it wasn't a large dose of a single drug in Daniel's system and given that it was a happy occasion and a time for celebration with him seeing his new sister, Dr. Wecht ruled out suicide. It was the combination of the three drugs that caused the cardiac dysrhythmia, which led to Daniel's death.

Dr. Wecht said he could only find one of the antidepressants, Lexapro, as being prescribed. He was able to trace that to Dr. Sandeep Kapoor in California. Dr. Kapoor told him that the prescription for Lexapro had been written for Daniel to help him deal with depression after he broke up with a girlfriend approximately four to five weeks before. The depression would have gotten bad mid-summer, around the same time that Anna had moved to the Bahamas with Howard K. Stern.

Dr. Wecht said he believed the other anti-depressant, Zoloft, had been prescribed by another doctor, he "just did not know who." Ray Martino, who Daniel was living with before his trip to the Bahamas that night, claims he found Zoloft in Daniel's belongings in California, two weeks after Daniel's death. The prescription was half full. According to Dr. Keith Eddleman at New York's Mt. Sinai Hospital, Zoloft and Lexapro are both "Seratonin Reuptake Inhibitors" and taking the two of them in combination would have a similar effect as taking a double dose of one of them. "Serious," he said. "But probably not in and of itself fatal. The methadone could have pushed those over the edge."

So, the big question is, where did the methadone come from, which Dr. Wecht says delivered the fatal blow. He also says it appears to have been ingested, not injected. Remember, Dr. Kapoor had just written a methadone prescription and shipped it to a pregnant "Vicky Marshall" (Anna Nicole's real name) only a few days before Daniel's death. Shortly after Anna's death, the website tmz.com released a photo showing methadone in her refrigerator. Eyewitnesses tell me they saw the drugs not only in Anna's personal refrigerator in her bedroom, but also multiple bottles in the main refrigerator in the kitchen.

According to Jack Harding, the private investigator Daniel spoke to, Daniel said Howard gave everyone drugs, "including me." But Daniel added he "got off of them," and was "now clean."

When Dr. Wecht spoke with Howard and his attorney after the autopsy, and told them that Daniel's death was caused by a lethal drug combination, he says Howard appeared to be "shocked and saddened by this event."

It is, as one medical examiner told me, possible that Howard gave Daniel the methadone and did not anticipate that Daniel would die.

Monday, September 18

Getty Images, the world's leading photo broker, sold all of Howard's photos of Daniel's last night alive to *In Touch Weekly* and *Entertainment Tonight* for reportedly upwards of $400,000. What Howard hadn't given to Getty Images was the gruesome last photos showing Daniel dead in Anna's arms. But knowing that several people had already seen them, he warned at least one friend "that if you hear about me taking those photos, here's why: Anna wanted me to take some pictures because she thought he'd come alive again like a prince."

That same night that Getty made the deal on the photos of Daniel with his new baby sister, *Entertainment Tonight* aired an interview with celebrity photographer Larry Birkhead, the man who claimed he was the father of Anna's newborn baby. "I've never had a person take off and run away from me, especially to another country," he said. "The reason why, I was told, she went to the Bahamas was, I guess if a baby is born in the Bahamas and the mother is a resident of the Bahamas, I think it would be harder for a father who wanted to participate in a baby's life to be able to do so."

Howard K. Stern said he was shocked and angered that Larry Birkhead would use the media to suggest things about Anna and her baby that weren't true, and he scheduled a media appearance for the following week on *Larry King Live* to say so.

Wednesday, September 20

Bahamas Chief Justice Sir Burton Hall issued a Supreme Court Memorandum, stripping magistrate Linda Virgill of the exclusive designation of "coroner" and abolishing the special "Coroner's Court." Linda Virgill was not unfamiliar with the cutthroat nature of Bahamian politics. Her husband, Charles Virgill, the former Bahamian Housing Minister and Free National Movement election campaign manager, had been shot to death in 1997 after disappearing from a party meeting kicking off the election campaign.

The Bahama Journal reported that Chief Justice Hall did not provide a reason for his decision to abolish the "Coroner's Court," effectively axing Linda Virgill from further investigating the "suspicious" death of Daniel Wayne Smith.

Howard K. Stern had gotten his wish: Linda Virgill had been "removed."

Thursday, September 21

Eleven days after his death in Anna's hospital room, Daniel's death certificate was issued on September 21, with the caveat "pending chemical analysis" on tissue samples that had already been taken. Though his body could now finally be lawfully buried, the funeral was still yet almost a full month away. There were apparently many issues that had to be resolved: including, where he would be buried and then how that would be paid for. Anna was living on the good graces of friends and a lot of IOUs.

Despite word of big money photo and media deals, Anna and Howard were having "financial problems." Apparently, the money wasn't coming in as fast as it was going out. Exactly where hundreds of thousands of dollars in photo rights and exclusive fees were going is still unclear. Ben Thompson and Ford Shelley told me they were paying many of Anna and Howard's expenses at that point, including buying their groceries and paying their utilities. Moe and other employees have said they weren't getting paid.

Howard, according to his own testimony after Anna's death, said he only had one client, Anna Nicole Smith. And after Daniel's death, his advisor role kicked into high gear. Decisions had to be made about their future, including where Daniel was going to be buried.

According to an interview Bahamian *Controversy TV* did with Haitian nanny Nadine Alexie, who was caring for Dannielynn at the time, Anna wanted Daniel to be buried in Texas, where he was born. Apparently, Howard quickly talked her out of it. Nadine explained in her broken English, "Howard said it will cost too much money to bury Daniel in Texas because there'll be lots of money for transportation ... And Anna said, 'I thought that whenever you [weren't] born in a country, you're not supposed to be buried in that country.' And Howard said, you know, it's okay. She can bury him right here in the Bahamas, that will cost them less money."

She also explained, "Anna didn't have too much money back then and the money she was collecting for selling the baby's picture ... that money wouldn't be enough to go and bury the boy down there in Texas."

Anna had also always said she wanted to be buried in Hollywood, near Marilyn Monroe. So, a few days after Daniel died, Ray Martino and Howard's mother, Broncha Machla Schwartzwald Stern, had gone looking for the appropriate place to bury celebrity Anna Nicole Smith's child in Hollywood, where he lived and Anna had become famous.

Marilyn Monroe is buried at Westwood Village Memorial Park in Los Angeles, according to *Forbes* magazine one of the "Top 10 of America's Best and Richest Cemeteries." Hidden behind towering high-rises that line the heavily trafficked Wilshire Boulevard, is this tiny cemetery near UCLA, which is the final resting spot of some of Hollywood's most famous stars. Besides Marilyn, Westwood Village is the home of the remains of Donna Reed, Natalie Wood, Eva Gabor, and Truman Capote. Martino and Howard's mother discovered that there were no empty spots available near Marilyn. Hugh Hefner had already bought the crypt next to his most famous centerfold for himself.

They settled on the Forest Lawn Cemetery in Glendale, California. The Forest Lawn Cemetery is also a "Hollywood" place to be buried. This cemetery of the stars is the final resting place of many A-listers, including Gracie Allen, Gene Autry, Lucille Ball, Bette Davis, Burt Convy, Liberace, and Telly Savalas.

Since they definitely wanted Daniel to be buried in Hollywood, Ray Martino and Howard's mother picked out a plot in Forest Lawn and had the contracts drawn. Forest Lawn just needed signatures and payment. Approximately one week later, Howard informed them and others that there was a change in plans. He called Ray Martino back in Los Angeles and announced, "We've decided to bury Danny here, and decided to live here."

Anna said she wanted Daniel to be near her.

America's most buxom troubled beauty decided she was going to live in the Bahamas for the rest of her life.

CHAPTER 4

Shopping

THE LACK OF MONEY WAS BECOMING A GROWING PROBLEM AS Anna and Howard dealt with their other worries. Daniel's death was weighing heavily on them both, and Larry Birkhead, one of Anna's old boyfriends, had graduated from threatening e-mails to media appearances, speaking ever more loudly that he was the father of Anna's newborn baby.

As for the claims of fatherhood, there was only so far they could run from the truth of DNA testing. But she certainly knew that what her ex-boyfriend Larry Birkhead was saying, was actually true. And in regards to money and favors, there is only so long that Anna could live on "I'm a celebrity" credit, depending on the kindness of friends and friendly new strangers to cut her a break. Anna was most likely unaware of the numerous IOUs that were stacking up and that many people, like bodyguard Moe Brighthaupt, remained unpaid.

Anna Nicole wasn't handling any money. She hadn't handled her money in years. That was Howard's job. Quethlie

Alexis and Nadine Alexie, two nannies working for Anna during the time, say that Anna clearly had a money shortage and that Howard would often put a stack of paperwork in front of Anna when she was heavily drugged and tell her to sign it. On several occasions the nannies heard Anna tell Howard that she couldn't read the papers, and he'd tell her to sign anyway. Howard signed most of the nannies' checks with the name "Vickie Lynn Marshall," and they claim that Dr. Khris Eroshevich, Anna's psychiatrist who often visited, also signed checks right in front of them the same way, using the signature "Vickie Lynn Marshall."

At least the nannies were being paid. Others were working without remuneration, biding their time and biting their tongues until the Marshall money came in. "I got there the day after Daniel died, September 11," bodyguard Moe Brighthaupt told Fox News. "And up to the day she died, I didn't get paid one cent to work with her. . . . She was going through a lot of legal problems, so you know, I didn't want to bug her with that."

Moe told the private investigators that at one point he knew Anna had several hundred thousand dollars in her safe in Los Angeles and believes that it was later moved to the Bahamas. Moe would see Howard pay "big wads of cash" all the time to people who'd come over to the house in the Bahamas. He saw "lots of money changing hands at that house." Howard told several close employees that there was no money, but promised there would be once Anna had finally won her battle against the family of her deceased billionaire husband.

According to Moe, Howard "took care of everything. Her money and her drugs." But Anna's live-in lawyer was also overseeing all the other lawyers who were handling the growing tangle of legal woes for the blonde star. In addition to the case that had been appealed all the way to the Supreme Court over the billion dollar fortune of J. Howard Marshall, the eighty-six-year-old man she had met while stripping, she had the Bahamas residency issues, the looming paternity suit, the "suspicious" death of her son, and, soon, a dispute with dear friends over the house she and Howard were living in.

The hole was getting deeper and deeper. Or the hill was becoming an insurmountable mountain.

• • •

It was Howard that was handling Anna's money as well as her career. He knew what was valuable about the Anna brand and what people wanted to see. And he was always trying to work every angle.

Anna and Howard's friend David Giancola, the producer of Anna's last film *Illegal Aliens*, told me, "Howard was always thinking like a businessman. His theory has always been 'make them pay.' Whenever anyone wanted to run even a clip of Anna, he'd always try to get some money from it, saying, 'if they are going to get ratings, we should get dollars.'"

After Daniel died, Howard was often seen chain smoking in the corner in the Horizons house, on secret phone calls and working on his computer a lot. But the tragedy was now making bankable news. The media and the public wanted, and was willing to pay for, access to Anna's pain, to know what she was going through, to see just how messy the life of America's favorite scarlet letter wearer had become.

Less than a week after Daniel's death, Howard had made the big-money deal with *In Touch* magazine. In addition, about four days after Howard closed the *In Touch* deal, a contract from *Entertainment Tonight* worth a purported million dollars arrived at their Horizons house. It was a contract that would give them money so that they could bury Daniel, climb out of mounting debt, and a deal that, Howard hoped, would give them some much-needed positive publicity.

Tuesday, September 26

Five days after Daniel's death certificate was issued, in advance of the photo shoot and splashy *Entertainment Tonight* exclusive, Howard appeared on *Larry King Live* with the promise of a major announcement.

Larry King first read a statement by Larry Birkhead: "I've been told by Anna Nicole Smith that I'm the father of her newborn child. I have proof of it. I've attended multiple doctors' appointments, participated in the planning of this child up until a minor disagreement more than midway through the pregnancy. In order to eliminate the back and forth claims regarding paternity, I am requesting that a DNA test take place in the U.S."

And then Howard fired back. "Well," he began. "I think you have to look at what his motives are and, you know, if he honestly believed that he was the father based on when the baby was born, he should have handled it appropriately.

"First, he should have waited until Daniel was put to rest," he continued, reminding millions of people that Daniel had not yet been buried more than two weeks after his death. "And, second, handle it through the proper channels, not through television and through the media. I mean for him to do that on *Entertainment Tonight* and, at the same time, send a slew of e-mails to Anna, it's just completely inappropriate."

It was an ironic statement considering Howard himself was sitting in a television studio, dealing with the situation "through television and through the media."

Regarding the slew of e-mails, apparently unbeknownst to Howard, Anna had been more than just getting e-mails from Larry Birkhead; she had also been speaking to him covertly on the phone and text messaging him, sometimes even using other people's cell phones. According to Anna's employee confidante, Larry Birkhead, the man claiming to be the father of her child, was secretly a part of her life even as late as January 2007. In fact, on Christmas Day 2006, Anna called Larry to tell him "the baby is beautiful" and "she loved him." After the conversation, Larry told people he was so happy to get the nice call.

"They used to talk on the phone," he said. "They would talk for hours. The minute Howard would come around, she would hang up."

But Howard K. Stern didn't know about the ongoing conversations and, in fact, spun a different story. "She never considered him a boyfriend," he said during the nationally televised interview. "Anna and I have been in a relationship and we love each other and it's been going on for a very long time and because of my relationship as her lawyer, we felt that it was best to keep everything hidden. And we've done a pretty good job of that."

Howard K. Stern announced, "I am the proud father."

• • •

Howard's announcement was a shock not only to America but also to most of Anna and Howard's friends. One of Howard's closest friends told me privately, "Since Howard came out on TV and said he's the dad, I was always suspicious of him. But I didn't want to get in the middle of it."

Peter Nygard, the billionaire fashion designer whom Anna

dated for three years in the late 1990s, said, "Howard was Anna's houseboy. She was clearly not interested in him."

"I bet the bank they never had sex," Ben Thompson told me. He, like Peter Nygard, was another boyfriend Anna had during the ten years she knew Howard. Thompson said Anna and Howard had separate bedrooms, even when they visited his family in South Carolina. "He was her personal valet," he said, "but never her lover. If he ever looked at her with lust, she would have clocked him."

Ben Thompson knew the two of them for years, and says he never saw Howard romantic with anyone. According to Jackie Hatten, Daniel's godmother, Anna Nicole told her, "Eeeew! I'd never sleep with Howard, if he's the last person on earth. He's gay!"

Ben Thompson says that Anna told him on numerous occasions, "Howard was repulsive to her." He also revealed to me startling conversations he had had directly with Anna and Howard, which show that Howard knew from the beginning that he was not the father of little Dannielynn. Ben divulged that these conversations happened "right before she left for the Bahamas and while in the Bahamas, when they were trying to get me to say I was the father of Anna's newborn."

In early summer of 2006, when Anna was around five months pregnant, Howard was "country shopping," according to friends. He wanted to find a locale that would be a good escape from looming paternity issues. Bahamian patrimonial law and the kind treatment of the rich and famous played into Howard and Anna's strategy when they were considering where to move.

An eyewitness says Howard, acting as Anna's attorney, called the Nassau law firm of Callender and Company. The eldest Callender established his practice in Nassau in the early 1900s. Since then, the name Callender has become synonymous with law in the Bahamas. Howard said that he was the attorney for Anna Nicole Smith and claimed that they were having trouble with the father of Anna's unborn baby.

"She doesn't want to be anywhere near the father," Howard told Bahamian attorney Michael Scott. "The father is threatening her. We want to make it difficult to have paternity proven. He's creating problems, and may be threatening her with alimony issues and other things. Is it [the Bahamas] a safe haven for us?"

The eyewitness to Howard's conversation told me "it was clear they were running away from the father and trying to get a legal opinion to make sure the Bahamas was the right place to escape their expected legal troubles." There was an orchestrated reason for their asylum in the Bahamas. "Howard specifically asked if the Bahamas was a suitable jurisdiction to avoid paternity issues."

"We need a friendly jurisdiction for our purpose," Howard reiterated to the Bahamian attorney. He then explained that they needed to be quick because the father was already beating the drum. He said that Anna needed to deliver the baby in the islands, as well as establish residency to protect Anna against stateside claims from the father.

Soon after the conversation, Howard decided that the Bahamas was a good choice.

"It was one big façade," said the eyewitness.

A month later they had packed up their life and moved to the Bahamas, but not before asking Ben Thompson if he'd be willing to be listed as the father of the baby.

"I can't," he said. "I've had a vasectomy."

"Is there any way that your vasectomy didn't work?" Anna pleaded.

"I know it worked," her friend said. "I was at the doctor's recently. Honey, I can't have kids. It's a matter of record. I can't be the father. It would be an obvious lie."

"Pleeeeease," Anna begged, putting on her little girl voice and pouting her lips.

"Let me think about it," Ben said, swayed by her beseeching. "But I don't think it's right."

As it turns out, the vasectomy wouldn't matter in the Bahamas. There, paternity law presumes that a male is recognized by law as the father of a child in several circumstances that would suit Anna's needs. Paternity in the Bahamas can be established if "the person marries the mother of the child after the birth of the child and acknowledges that he is the natural father." Or, if marriage is too "confining," the father of a child can be the man who "was cohabitating with the mother of the child in a relationship of some permanence at the time of the birth of the child."

And if marriage or even living together is not desired, paternity may be established if the man has "acknowledged in proceedings for registration of the child . . . that he is the father of the child." In other words, if a woman names a man as the father, and the man says he is, he is recognized as the father under Bahamian law. The laws are so loose that many Bahamian men joke that basically anybody can be a "father."

The law says if the paternity is questioned or challenged, upon appeal, the court may seek to obtain blood tests of "such persons as the court specifies," but the person named can refuse to submit to the tests. Then, "the court may draw such inferences as it thinks appropriate."

Anna just needed to get her permanent Bahamian residency to avoid any subpoenas or demands that might come from Larry Birkhead and the American courts, or so she thought.

The philosophy of the Bahamian government on immigration, like paternity laws, was relatively amenable to her needs. If you want to live in the Bahamas, you must be of "good character." Messy television moments could be overlooked, as long as the applicant didn't have a criminal record. The applicant should be prepared to show evidence of financial support. Even though she did not have a lot of money at the time, she did have a lucrative contract with TrimSpa and she was a big name star.

But the best attraction to Anna's Bahamavention was that "accelerated consideration" is given to applications for annual or permanent residence to major international investors who have residences valued at $500,000 or more.

Anna had the country. Now, she just needed the house.

• • •

Anna Nicole had earlier vacationed in the Bahamas with former boyfriend and billionaire fashion mogul Peter Nygard in the late 1990s. Bahamians have made celebrities feel welcome for years, which is why it has become a destination playground for those with money and, like "Anna Nicole Smith," with marquee names. Peter owns a luxurious private resort in the Bahamas called Nygard Cay. It is its own fantasy island, with cabanas on stilts, views of the ocean from every cabana, and the perfect place to escape.

Anna and Peter had met at one of the Academy Awards' parties he throws annually in Los Angeles. She was with another guy, but she paid attention to Peter all night and they exchanged numbers. This encounter resulted in Anna and

Peter dating on and off from 1997 to 2000, and Anna becoming one of his models, posing in his catalogs and going on trips with him.

"Anna called me twice before she came to the Bahamas, around June of 2006," Peter Nygard said. "She told me she may be going there, and told me she was looking for a house."

"Is it okay if I stay with you as a back-up?" she asked Peter. "If I can't find a place right away?"

She told Peter she would love to go there with him again, and asked if he'd take her there almost immediately on his private plane. "I told her I couldn't go right then because of work," he said.

"She was truly a sweetheart," Peter told me. "One of the most fun, charming people you would ever meet. But she had such a problem with drugs. I thoroughly enjoyed her when she was sober, but I was so depressed when I saw her so drunk and out of it." Peter says there were always lots of prescription drugs around her, and she always wanted more. At one point while they were dating, Peter had to put her in her own room—a separate room from his—because she was so out of control with her drug use. He had someone assigned to watch her on his large property in Nassau because he was scared she'd trip or fall down the stairs and hurt herself. Peter broke up with Anna because he says he wouldn't go along with her on her drug issues. After he told her, "You are not going to self destruct on my watch," he had put distance between them.

Even if Anna couldn't stay with Peter, she had another option that proved to be even better for avoiding paternity issues. South Carolinian Ben Thompson wouldn't readily agree to claim he was the father of Anna's baby, but he did say yes to letting them stay at his luxurious Bahamian waterfront estate, Horizons. Worth more than a half million dollars, the real estate criteria for expedited Bahamian residency, Horizons would be the perfect house for them until Ben wanted it back.

After moving to the Bahamas, Anna's need for a father had grown in direct relation to her growing belly, and as her due date approached, she again began asking Ben Thompson to let her put his name down on the birth certificate. "She kept urging me to do it," Ben explained. "And I kept telling her and Howard that I can't be the dad because I had the vasectomy. The odds are 1 in 10 million, and I didn't want to lie on paper."

Anna and Ben had several discussions about it. She told him that Howard really wanted to be listed as the father and was very disappointed that he was not going to be listed on the birth certificate. Ben surmises that Howard clearly wanted to be tied to her. Ben finally said to her, "I'm here to help you in any way I can. You know I love you, but I can't do this."

Ben repeated to Howard that he couldn't do it. "I can't put a lie down on paper," he reiterated.

Anna Nicole did not list a father in the first version of Dannielynn's birth certificate, telling their close friends that she wasn't sure whom she wanted to put down as father. "They both made statements that they knew Howard was not the father," an eyewitness said. "We all knew Larry Birkhead was the dad."

Toward the end of September as Larry Birkhead began to get more vocal in his claims of fatherhood, Anna told Ben that if he wouldn't say he was the father, that Howard had offered to do it. Perhaps she hoped that would push Ben towards "yes." He didn't bite. After a final discussion took place in the Bahamas between Ben, Howard, and Anna at the Horizons house, Ben refused a final time to list himself as father.

"Anna is going to be very disappointed with you," Howard told him.

Ben left the next day and returned to the States. A few days later, Howard came on *Larry King Live*, saying he's the dad and shocking the world.

Larry King Live, *September 26, 2006*

"Dannielynn is the first name and Hope is the middle name and where that comes from is that Daniel used to call Anna or his mom 'Mamma Lynn,'" Howard announced like the proud father, the one he was claiming to be. "I'll tell you, our baby is one ray of hope and it's the one thing that's really keeping her going and through it all, even with all the pain she has been a great mom, a very attentive mom and she's always by Dannielynn's side."

"By the way," Larry King asked. "Have there been any DNA tests taken?

"Proud father," Stern answered.

"What?" King asked, confused by the "Who's on First?" exchange.

"I said proud father."

"Were DNA tests taken?" Larry repeated.

"Well, based on the timing of when the baby was born there really is no doubt in either of our minds," Howard said with the verbal acuity of a legally trained professional.

"Did Daniel know that you were the father?"

"He did. He did," Howard said.

But Daniel knew Howard wasn't the father. According to a close friend of Howard's, in the spring of 2006 Daniel and Anna told him Larry Birkhead was the dad. Larry Birkhead has also confirmed that Daniel knew he was the father and that they had had conversations about it. According to this friend who talked to her regularly until her death, by early 2007 Anna just wanted to take the DNA test and get it over with. Let the whole world know it was Larry's kid and end the charade, she confided to friends. "But several days after she told me that," one friend said, "Ron Rale came out and said he is not allowing her to take the DNA test, that he's against it." Privately, Howard and Ron Rale were in agreement. "But she definitely planned at some point to have the baby in California," the friend said. "She made a room for the baby with beautiful granite floors at her house in Los Angeles."

• • •

"If it got to a legal case," Larry King asked Howard, "if supposedly there were lawsuits involved, would you take a DNA?"

"Yes," Howard said. "At this point if he was able to file a lawsuit and do it, I don't know why he hasn't done it through legal means. I don't understand, you know, why he would choose to go through the media to do what he's done. But at this point I'm not going to do him any favors . . . . It's unforgivable to me the way that he—with everything that we're going through right now—that he would go to the media and not wait until Daniel has been put to rest."

According to a close friend, in addition to the financial issues of having Daniel's funeral in Texas or California, Howard told Anna she could not risk going back to the United States to bury Daniel because of the impending paternity issues. Howard helped Anna come to terms with the reality that Daniel had to be buried in the Bahamas, the place he had told Ray Martino he never wanted to live. When they discovered that a mausoleum in the Bahamas was cost prohibitive, they settled on a gravesite where, planning ahead, they could get four plots side by side—

one for Daniel, one for Anna, one for Howard, and one for "their new baby together," Dannielynn.

When Larry King asked Howard about a tabloid report that Anna Nicole needed money and therefore sold photos of Daniel and his baby half-sister to pay for the funeral, Howard responded, "When we had all the media outcry after Daniel passed, there's literally been photographers camped across the street, driving back and forth, camera crews. And we decided that if we release those images, which told a story of a joyous night that it was going to be a good thing and we were going to do it to create a Daniel Wayne Smith Charitable Foundation. So she hasn't profited from those images . . . Obviously, the funeral is going to take place long before any money comes from that."

In that night's highly talked about interview, Howard said Anna picked the Bahamas "to get away from the media and to start a new life" and to give her daughter "a chance to live a normal life." The next months of their "normal" life would get even weirder. Before they would get around to burying Daniel, Anna and Howard would do a "photo-op" commitment ceremony for *People* magazine. And, after they'd bury him in a heartbreaking, surreal funeral, they'd sell "exclusive" interviews to *Entertainment Tonight* for a reported one million dollars that would include Howard's dramatic video footage of her C-section, Anna's tears over Daniel, and her venomous, heavily medicated, diatribe of hatred towards her mother.

Anna's life was anything but normal. And the strangest and possibly most deceptive episodes were yet to come.

CHAPTER 5

Committed and Buried in Debt

ANNA WAS SLEEPING A LOT. AND WHEN SHE WASN'T SLEEPING she was crying. The death of her son was haunting her. Though now a confusion of memories clouded by drugs and the blur of tears, she knew Daniel's death was real. She had a certificate saying so, and his decomposing body was awaiting burial in a Bahamian morgue. During her lucid moments, the recollections of the hours around his death deeply troubled her.

She told several employees, who have gone on record, that she was afraid Howard may have had something to do with Daniel's death. Quethlie Alexis and Nadine Alexie, two of Anna's Haitian nannies, gave sworn affidavits to Bahamian attorneys on December 4, 2006, in anticipation of being called as witnesses for the inquest into Daniel's death. They had made some highly charged accusations about Anna Nicole, Howard K. Stern, and events in the Horizons house on Eastern Road. They also went on Bahamian television saying that they are fearful for their lives because they discovered that

Howard K. Stern wanted information about them and where they live.

Quethlie Alexis, a thirty-seven-year-old married mother of one child, came to help Anna as the nursery maid and nanny for Anna's expected daughter on September 4, just three days before the birth. She says that the same day she met Anna, Anna told her she had no one to help her. "Where your family?" she asked in her broken English, since she speaks primarily Creole, a French dialect.

Anna replied that her mother wasn't in the Bahamas, or any family for that matter. Howard is "the lawyer," she said, pointing to him. He was in the Bahamas to "help her." Anna told the nanny that her boyfriend was away. And, according to the nanny, the situation in the house was not good. "Anna never talk to Howard," she said. Regarding the bedrooms where they slept, she said, "Separate."

"Notwithstanding the generally disreputable and unsuitable household in which I worked," Quethlie swore in her written statement, "My only concern was to do my absolute best to look after Dannielynn." She worked with Anna tending to the newborn, eight a.m. until ten p.m. seven days a week until Monday, November 27 . . . when everything changed.

"The whole domestic regime for Dannielynn is wild and unpredictable and her feeding is improper," Quethlie said in her sworn affidavit. "In addition, Ms. Marshall takes daily a lot of mood altering substances, with the result that she spends a lot of time asleep or resting in bed, and when she is up and about, her mood swings are extreme, and are very unsettling and I am therefore concerned for the baby's welfare."

Given Anna's state, the baby spent most of her time bonding with Quethlie and the two grew very close. Anna accused Quethlie of wanting Dannielynn to think of Quethlie as her mother rather than Anna. (A charge that Quethlie vehemently denies.) Anna put her concern very bluntly one day: "If I ever hear Dannielynn call you 'mummy,' I will have to shoot you." Quethlie says that "given Ms. Marshall's state of mind and general behavior, that I believed her."

She, however, continued her duties as nursery maid and nanny until the end of November, the day that a new washing machine was delivered to the Horizons house.

The new washing machine was fancy. It was a front-loading machine with a lot more switches than Ms. Alexis was accustomed, and she couldn't find the user manual. Anna, susceptible to remarkable mood swings and a quick temper, was livid and accused Quethlie of losing it. In a rage, Anna fired her on the spot.

Nadine Alexie, Quethlie's thirty-two-year-old sister-in-law and mother of two, was the "assistant baby minder" during the period, taking over from her sister-in-law at ten o'clock each night and staying until she was relieved in the morning. She signed a sworn affidavit saying that all Quethlie Alexis's charges were true. Despite this incident with the washing machine and what they believed were other drug induced outbursts, the nannies say Anna deep down was a very kind person. And they feel the real reason they were fired was because Howard K. Stern felt they knew too much, saw too much.

Both the nannies have repeatedly said that they overheard Anna telling Howard K. Stern around the time of Daniel's funeral: "You did this! You killed him! You caused this!" And that they had also heard Anna scream at him: "Get out of here! Just wait for the inquest!"

Wayne Munroe, Howard's Bahamian attorney, told me that the nannies were fired because "they were incompetent and insubordinate." When I asked him about their comments relating to Howard and Daniel's death, he said, "I don't expect anything more from ungrateful people."

But other employees have corroborated many of the nannie's sworn accusations. In fact, the employee confidante told me that Anna said that since she was heavily sedated she never really found out what happened, so she didn't know what to think. "But she thought there was something behind it, that it was strange that when Daniel came he was in good spirits, healthy, and then he just dropped dead.

"Someone poisoned him or give him drugs or something," she pointedly told him. "He didn't do drugs.

"Anna had a feeling that something went down," her employee said. "She repeated a couple of times that when Daniel came into the hospital he was okay, then 'Howard went to get something to eat and when he ate the food he just crapped out.'" And then she burst into tears and ran back to her room where she cried herself to sleep.

"She was afraid of Howard," he said. "You have to understand he had a strong hold on her. She didn't want to take any chances. He played a big role. She was scared and she didn't know what to do."

And, he says, the drugs were bad—both before Daniel's death when she was pregnant and after Daniel's death when she was not. He said he saw Anna using numerous drugs, including both methadone and cocaine while pregnant. "Every other day Howard would give her a little snort in the nose and get her high . . . Howard wanted to control her. He wanted her to get high and stay high. He'd say come get your medicine."

Anna would sweat a lot. She would suddenly break into cold sweats. "He was pushing her, until he couldn't push no more," he said. "He was killing her slowly." Bottles of methadone were, he says, kept on the left side of the refrigerator in her room. He says he saw her get injections in the arm both during and after her pregnancy. "Howard was doing it," he said. She'd take it every day, as well as numerous other prescription drugs that were often ground up and mixed into a glass of grapefruit juice.

This employee, like numerous others, also told me that Anna and Howard were having a tough time paying people. "I got paid the first month," he said. "But then I wasn't paid for four months. Other people weren't paid, lots of people. I guess there was no money. I wasn't there for the money. I was there for her. Money would come later. I'd spend my own money to make sure stuff was put in the refrigerator. I've never seen her with money. I think they got broke somewhere down the line."

Anna rarely left the house. Her trusted employee said she tried to outwardly put on a smile, but deep down she was hurting. "She put on a front a lot, but not with me. I knew something was going on . . . . He didn't want her to go anywhere, to see anybody. Mentally and physically controlling her. He just kept her in the house."

That is until it was time for a paid photo opportunity. In that case, the whole world could see her.

Thursday, September 28, 2006

The "bride" wore a white dress and carried a bouquet of red roses. The "groom" wore a black suit with a white shirt. It wasn't a real wedding with a marriage certificate or anything. Anna Nicole Smith and Howard K. Stern held an informal commitment ceremony floating in the waters off the coast of the Bahamas aboard *Margaritaville*, a 41-foot catamaran.

Michael Scott, one of their growing entourage of attorneys, told the media, "They needed a little adrenaline boost because things have been so hectic and devastating in their life recently." Perhaps more than an adrenaline boost, it was the financially bankable shots that would bring the couple an injection of cash that they desperately needed to keep their life afloat.

The "ceremony" was decidedly low key and simple. Anna Nicole was barefooted and wearing fake eyelashes that looked like she had a black moth wing stuck atop each eyelid. A cross necklace was nestled into her cleavage and her face was puffy. Though not a real wedding, she and Howard exchanged vows and temporary rings in front of a Baptist minister, as well as a small group of friends and beautiful Dannielynn, Anna Nicole's newborn daughter.

According to the press release, the couple dispatched to the media, they had "escaped their house" at three o'clock in the morning "and boarded a boat to quietly sail the ocean around Nassau . . . on a clandestine sail to recapture simple pleasures—fresh salt air on the face, a sunrise on the ocean, and wind in their hair. And then a good thing happened: during the sail, Anna Nicole Smith and Howard K. Stern made a commitment before God to be there for one another, to be each other's strength during this difficult time."

The release further said, "By mid-morning, helicopters flew overhead, speed boats approached, and camera-equipped scuba divers invaded what had been an otherwise perfect moment of peace, solitude, and hope. The event was intended to be totally private between two adults deeply in love with each other and needing simple reassurances that they could count on one another through life's ups and downs. The outing was never expected to be shared with anyone other than Howard,

Anna, [her newborn daughter] Dannielynn Hope and a few close friends and family."

• • •

After the ceremony, they landed on the island of Sandy Cay and the newly committed couple took the plunge into the temperate waters off the coast of the island. "Howard and Anna were both crying and kissing and holding hands," friend and former "Dynasty" actor John James told *People* magazine. The fifteen or so guests celebrated with champagne, apple cider, and Anna's favorite food, Kentucky Fried Chicken, which had been brought over for the occasion by sailboat.

But rather than being an outing that was, as their press release stated, "never expected to be shared with anyone," the bittersweet "wedding" photos of the whole affair and story were conveniently given to and sold by photo broker Getty Images to *People* magazine for a reported one million dollars.

Michael Scott, the attorney who had become their de facto Bahamian spokesperson in the aftermath of Daniel's death, towed the party line by announcing to the press, "This was intended to be a lift to steel them for Daniel's funeral." But behind the scenes, Michael Scott had vehemently argued against doing the ceremony. When Howard told the attorneys working with him and Anna that he wanted to do a commitment ceremony, they strongly advised him against it, saying they knew it would hurt Anna especially in the public's perception if they were seen selling their story and frolicking on a boat before her son was even buried.

That wasn't the only moneymaking idea the couple had around a wedding that was in questionable taste. According to the website TMZ, Anna Nicole and Howard were shopping a reality show featuring Anna's quest to find a husband, similar in concept to VH1's "Flavor of Love." Their production partner in the deal was Hallock Healey Entertainment, producers of "Breaking Up with Shannen Doherty," the "$25 Million Dollar Hoax," and the ironically titled "Who's Your Daddy?" In the 2005 Fox reality TV special, a grown adoptee, who happens to be a stunning blonde actress named "T.J." who also had played a stripper, had to choose her biological father from a panel of eight men.

Anna's show would have had men, "young and old, of different ethnicities and orientations," vying for Anna's affections. The "winner" would have gotten to marry her.

Although their commitment ceremony was officiated by the Baptist minister, no marriage certificate was issued, leading many to speculate that the "commitment" was certainly more for show than it was for substance. Had they actually wanted to get a marriage license, it is a relatively easy process in the Bahamas, much easier, in fact, than getting permanent residency on the island. It's a $40.00 fee with no blood test and only requires that both parties be in the Bahamas at the time of application. The two would have had to provide a form of identification and apply during business hours Monday through Friday at the nearby Office of the Registrar General in Nassau. The only other thing they would have needed was a copy of the death certificate for J. Howard Marshall, since Anna Nicole was widowed.

If Anna and Howard had wanted to go that route, it would have been entirely possible. But they didn't.

After the ceremony, Howard blocked outraged attorney Michael Scott and his co-counsel Tracy Ferguson from seeing Anna at the house. Michael Scott sent a note to Howard and Anna reminding them that too much time was passing after Daniel's death without proper burial and that it didn't look good. Arrangements for the next deal, the exclusive on Anna's C-section birth and Anna talking about Daniel's death, were being worked out with *Entertainment Tonight*. A person privy to the behind the scenes negotiations said, "After Anna and Howard were officially cleared to have Daniel buried, he laid there while they worked out their deals. It was disgusting, but it happened."

The week after the commitment ceremony, Michael Scott announced he was withdrawing as her counsel. "A disagreement on a commercial transaction made it difficult for us to remain as counsel," Scott told the Associated Press. He was very bothered by the *People* magazine pictorial and the fact that the event was held prior to making funeral arrangements for Daniel.

As of June 2007 there remained a $113,000 unpaid bill for Callender & Co.'s legal services.

October 2, 2006

The Monday following Anna Nicole and Howard's Bahamian commitment ceremony, the baby drama kicked into high gear. Larry Birkhead officially filed his paternity suit against Anna Nicole Smith, requesting a judge to order Anna Nicole to return "their" daughter Dannielynn to California and immediately submit to a paternity test. He also demanded that both mother and daughter be tested for drugs.

Larry Birkhead's high-powered attorney Debra Opri said they were asking for legal and physical custody of the little girl Larry vehemently claimed to be his biological daughter. Opri said that Birkhead is "a first time father and he is responding to allegations made by attorney Howard K. Stern on behalf of

Anna Nicole Smith, and believes beyond any doubt that he is the father."

Larry Birkhead appeared with me live on MSNBC's *Scarborough Country* that night and declared that he was definitely the father. He made some shocking allegations and claimed that Anna Nicole deliberately fled to the Bahamas to avoid custody and visitation issues. It was an eye-opener and it went like this:

RITA COSBY, HOST: We have just learned that, in just the last few hours, Larry Birkhead has filed suit against Anna Nicole Smith and is demanding that a paternity test be ordered to prove his claim that he's the father. Sources tell me that the court filing is explosive, Joe, with some very damning claims against Anna Nicole Smith.

I've learned that it alleges Anna Nicole Smith was taking methadone and that Howard K. Stern, her attorney, was allegedly facilitating her prescription drug habit, that she fled to the Bahamas after Birkhead suggested that the baby be tested for drugs, and that the filing says Howard K. Stern is claiming paternity for his own financial gain.

And this one is a real shocker: It alleges that Anna Nicole previously tried to get another man, a third guy, to claim it was his baby several months ago. But get this: That man had a vasectomy.

Joining me now exclusively is the man who filed this legal action, the man who says he's the real father of Anna Nicole Smith's new baby girl, Larry Birkhead. Larry, why are you taking this legal action now?

LARRY BIRKHEAD, CLAIMS HE'S THE FATHER OF ANNA NICOLE'S BABY: Well, I have to say, Rita, I was outraged and angry over Howard K. Stern's remarks on *Larry King Live*, where he claimed to be the father of my baby girl. And that really upset me, and I was outraged that he tried to hoodwink the American public—and Larry King, as well—into thinking and believing his story, which was filled with inconsistencies. And it lacked coherency. And it was just outrageous.

COSBY: You know, by doing this action, it appears that you feel she's intentionally fleeing to the Bahamas so you can't be a part of this baby's life. Is that how you feel? And how so?

BIRKHEAD: I feel that she has deliberately fled to the Bahamas to avoid any talks of custody and visitation. And this was all a highly orchestrated event between herself and her attorney, Howard K. Stern. And I feel that it has to be stopped and the truth needs to be told to the American public that I am the father of this child and all of Howard Stern's lies need to stop right now.

COSBY: You know, these allegations against Anna Nicole that I'm told by other sources are in the lawsuit filing are very strong, including the allegation of a drug addiction, these allegations against Anna Nicole, and that the baby may be damaged.

I spoke with your attorney, Debra Opri, obviously very well known. She's represented a lot of high-profile folks before you. And she had a pretty strong statement I want to show. This is what she

said to me. She said, "The public will be very surprised when they learn the details of the lifestyle
this baby is going to be faced with if she remains in
the current situation."

Do you believe that the baby's health is at risk,
that you're doing what's best for the baby now?

BIRKHEAD: Well, I'll let my attorney, you know, stick
with the statement that my attorney gave, but I will
say that I'm fighting for what I believe in, and that's
that I am the father of my baby girl. And I want her
to return to the States so that I can maintain a relationship with her and have a relationship with her.

Right now, I have no rights, no visitation, no
rights whatsoever. They were all stripped from me.
And again, this was orchestrated between herself
and the attorney, and I think that it's time to get to
the bottom of it.

COSBY: Is there any way Howard K. Stern, who went
on national television last week . . .

BIRKHEAD: There is absolutely no way that Howard
Stern is the father of this child. He knows it; I know
it. And that's all there is to it.

He challenged me on live television to get an
attorney, and so I have taken him up on his offer.
And it's time to get to the bottom of it, and we will
soon see all the lies surrounding this circus that
he's taken and he's made out of my birth of my
baby daughter.

COSBY: You know, in the court filing, I understand from
other sources outside of you and your attorney—I

understand that Anna Nicole was pregnant with another baby of yours but miscarried last year. Is that true?

BIRKHEAD: Well, I'll let the—I think that will come out in time. And I'd rather not comment on that, you know, at this time.

COSBY: What do you want to say about your credibility, because he's attacked your credibility? And why are you speaking here tonight?

BIRKHEAD: Well, again, it was important for me to get, you know, to the bottom of this whole thing, the circus that they've created, and also just to let people know that, you know, I am a credible person. I was told I was the father. I've been through all of these motions and emotions to prepare for fatherhood. And I think this is just an absolute crime what has been done to me, and I'm ready to fight for my daughter.

COSBY: At the end of the day, you believe you will be . . . 100 percent?

BIRKHEAD: One hundred and ten percent.

The following day, Ron Rale, one of Anna's ever-expanding cadre of attorneys fired back: "The truth will be known. Justice will be served."

"Dannielynn's" birth certificate was redone and Stern was added. According to Bahamian birth certificate number 14598, Howard K. Stern was the proud father. Stern's last name was listed as the baby's last name, even though they were not le-

88

gally married, even by Bahamian standards. According to Milton Evans, a well-known Bahamian lawyer, "The baby will only take on the father's name if he swears in an affidavit or signifies to the registrar that he is the father, and is prepared for his name to appear on the birth certificate. The mother will also have to be present and confirm that he is the father. So, based on their joint declaration to the birth records officer, that decision will be made to put the name on the certificate as Stern."

Debra Opri was immediately prepared to file a fraud action against Stern on behalf of her client, Larry Birkhead.

Interestingly, the rest of Dannielynn Hope Marshall Stern's name was all about tribute: to J. Howard Marshall as the wealthy deceased husband, to Daniel as the dead old brother, to Lynn, her mother's "real life" middle name, and, most of all, proclaimed "Hope" for the future because the present was nothing but a sea of despair.

October 7, 2006

While Anna remained in seclusion in the Bahamas and Daniel's body awaited proper burial, his friends and family, including his grief-stricken father, Billy Smith, gathered at the First Baptist Church in Anna Nicole's hometown of Mexia, Texas, for a memorial service. Giant green cutouts of the Ninja Turtles greeted about fifty relatives and friends as they arrived at the church to remember the life of the special twenty-year-old.

Relatives remembered that he loved to play a Texas cowboy. Anna's friend and Daniel's godmother, Jackie Hatten, said that Daniel was a kind young man who kept his nose clean. "Daniel was sweet, sensitive, and very respectful," she told me. "He never cursed, rarely drank, and never wanted to do drugs. I don't think he ever even smoked a cigarette."

October 19, 2006

Under the blue but slightly cloudy, October Bahamian sky, a dark gold hearse, followed by a procession of three white limousines, slowly made its way down John F. Kennedy Drive to Lakeview Memorial Gardens and Mausoleum in Nassau. The gold hearse carried the body of Daniel Wayne Smith to his final resting place on the Bahamian Island.

Upon arrival, the mahogany casket carrying the body of young Daniel was pulled from the hearse and carried past six security officers into the cemetery. As ten more officers, dressed discreetly as guests, stood guard, two dozen invited guests or so made their way into the graveyard and stood quietly around the grave, highlighted only by the shadow cast by a green tent, which had been erected for the private ceremony.

Positioned in front of a white pavilion known as the Citadel, the guests at the graveside service looked strangely out of place in their dark attire on such a beautiful, and warm, Bahamian day. Daniel's sister, six-week-old Dannielynn, was also in attendance, fawned over by family friends and tended to by Anna Nicole's personal assistant. Anna arrived in a black dress and veil created for her by couture designer and close friend Pol Atteu, who had also designed the dress for her commitment ceremony to Howard K. Stern.

Anna Nicole Smith was inconsolable. She had real problems accepting that Daniel was gone. In fact, Ben Thompson said the day Daniel died in the hospital, a few hours after she was home and her sedation drugs wore off, Anna had walked out of the bedroom into the living room where Ben and Howard were. "Where's Daniel?" she asked. "Where's he at?" Then, she pointed at his suitcase and said, "There's his bag."

"It stunned us," Ben Thompson remembers. "She still thought Daniel was alive. We looked at each other and took her into the bedroom. Howard told her what happened and it was like Daniel died all over again."

• • •

Just before Daniel's funeral was to begin, Anna demanded that the casket be opened. In front of the small crowd, she sobbed uncontrollably and reached into the coffin, grabbing onto Daniel's body clad in his favorite clothing: a pair of jeans, t-shirt, and a trucker hat. She was hugging her dead son, clinging to him. It was an extraordinarily anguishing moment to see a mother in such pain.

Daniel had been dead for thirty-nine days.

• • •

Even more shocking perhaps, Quethlie Alexis and Nadine Alexie told investigators that when Howard tried to console Anna and gently get her to release Daniel's body, she looked right at Howard and screamed, "You caused this! You did this. Get away from me, you bastard!" It was a surprising and uncomfortable moment for the small crowd.

"If Daniel has to be buried," she cried, "I want to be buried with him!" She was trying to go down with Daniel into the grave right then and had to be pulled from his dead body.

The tragic wailing and crying coming from within the tent could be heard throughout the cemetery, drowning out much of Howard K. Stern's eulogy in honor of Daniel. Anna had asked Daniel's friends to write letters that were placed in the casket, along with a photo of her with Daniel, and a rosary that had been blessed by the Pope. Those present shared words of love, sadness, and grief, but Anna was absolutely overwhelmed by her loss. Howard K. Stern would say in a statement released after the funeral, "Anna Nicole laid her son to rest today. It was the most difficult day of her entire life."

The program given out at the service was filled with pictures of Anna and Daniel saying he was like "a comet, blazing across the evening sky" who "died too soon like a rainbow fading." Also included was a personal note from Anna to her son. "My dearest son Daniel," Anna wrote, "You were my rock. You were the only one who could keep me solid. Why God took you away from me now I do not understand. Perhaps someday I will. It is so hard to think of you, but I do every second."

One hundred thirty-four days later she would be by his side.

CHAPTER 6

Residency and Eviction

THE DAY AFTER ANNA NICOLE SMITH FINALLY BURIED HER SON
Daniel, an attorney representing Ben Thompson hand-delivered
a letter to Horizons, the house in which she and Howard were
living and Ben said he still owned. The letter notified her that
she had to vacate the residence by October 31.

It wasn't unexpected. Ben Thompson had been asking
Anna for weeks to begin making the promised payments toward the $900,000 mortgage on the house. "I don't want to
embarrass her or humiliate Anna," Ben said. "I just need my
money, or collateral, back." Ben said he did sign the deed over
to Anna Nicole Smith on the Horizons house. He was allowing her to use the title so that she could get the expedited
residency she desperately needed to protect herself from ex-
boyfriend Larry Birkhead's paternity claims. But, Ben says,
the plan was always for them to make payments on the house,
which he never received.

Anna seemed to know for some time that she owed money

to Ben Thompson. The day after Howard K. Stern appeared on *Larry King Live* blasting Larry and proclaiming that he, Howard, was the "proud father" of Dannielynn, an e-mail was sent from Anna Nicole's e-mail account to Ben Thompson's work e-mail address. According to Fox News, which obtained the series of e-mails, the September 29 message, with its misspellings and grammatical errors, said in part, "i have NO MONEY, here I cant even berry my son! . . . and they want to do this to me make me sign a mortgage on my house my son isn't even taken care of!!!!!!!"

The next day, another e-mail from Anna's account arrived in Ben Thompson's inbox. It said, "send the note, i will sign it. Anna." And then, four days later, on October 4, another saying, "please don't worry im working on getting the money for the house!"

Money. Though big money deals had been made for photos and exclusives—for hundreds of thousands of dollars, more money than many people will make in a lifetime—the actual funds had either been slow in coming or, possibly, going elsewhere for other uses.

• • •

Before Anna came to the Bahamas, she and Howard had retained the well-connected law firm of Callender and Co. in Nassau to help assist her through the residency process, which would give Larry Birkhead more hurdles to jump in his paternity claims. Through Callender, she and Howard were introduced to Bahamas Immigration Minister Shane Gibson, and a friendship blossomed between Anna and Shane Gibson.

A statement Howard K. Stern gave to the Bahamian *Tribune* said, "We actually met Minister Gibson for the first time after Tracy Ferguson of Callender and Co. advised us to do so. After

our initial meeting we shared a cordial, but not close, relationship with Minister Gibson prior to the death of Anna Nicole's
son Daniel."

Anna Nicole's residency certificate was fast-tracked at
lightning speed and, according to the *Tribune*, it was received
in an "absolutely impossible" timeframe and under questionable circumstances. It is highly unusual to get residency ap-
proved within three weeks. Many people have been waiting
for years. Virtually everyone in the Bahamas felt Anna got
special treatment.

After her application had been submitted on Friday, August 11, an Immigration Department official called the following Monday, August 14, to set up an interview for the next day
at Horizons. Callender & Co. only learned her residency had
been granted when an exuberant Anna called her attorneys'
offices on September 20 and asked her attorney to bring a
$10,000 check to Horizons at seven o'clock that night.

Anna had gotten a call from Shane Gibson directly. He told
her the news and said he was coming by that night. When
attorney Tracy Ferguson arrived at Anna's house to give her
the check, Immigration Minister Shane Gibson was there. It
was clear to an eyewitness that Anna thought she was paying
Shane directly and questioned why the check was written to
the government instead.

According to the *Tribune*, the next day, September 21, the
Permanent Secretary called Callender & Co. and asked Michael Scott, Anna's attorney and a senior partner at the firm,
to send Immigration the $10,000 check for residency. The sec-
retary was surprised to learn that the firm had never received
the approval letter and that the check had been delivered the
night before directly to Minister Gibson. It was then suggested
that she ask the minister's office, where the check was eventu-

ally discovered. Within 24 hours, what looked like a quickly written letter was delivered to Callender & Co.

There were allegations made that expensive gifts were given to Shane Gibson, including a Rolex watch. He denied the accusations with carefully chosen words, repeatedly saying that there were "never any gifts for favors." According to bodyguard Moe Brighthaupt, the one thing Anna definitely gave Shane Gibson was naming him the godfather of Dannielynn.

"It was when Daniel passed away that we really came to know Minister Gibson," Howard K. Stern said in his statement to the *Tribune*. "The entire Gibson family—not just Minister Gibson—provided a great deal of emotional support to both Anna Nicole and I during a very difficult period."

Shortly after her death, photos of Anna and Immigration Minister Shane Gibson in bed together—clothed but fawning over each other—would be splashed across the front page of the Bahamian *Tribune* newspaper and led to Gibson's resignation. Howard had, of course, taken the photos. In addition, what transpired between the two of them between August and February would make Anna Nicole, the Playboy Playmate and reality TV star, Bahamas' number one election year political topic and was believed by many to have contributed to the defeat of the ruling party.

• • •

Shane Gibson's father, King Eric Gibson, a famed Bahamian steel drum musician, and Brigitte, his common-law wife, as well as Gerlene Gibson, his ex-wife, and several other members of the Gibson family found ways to assist Anna. "She was searching," King Eric told me. "She was always searching for a home that she never had. And she found it. We just so happened to be there."

"We didn't put any demands on her," acknowledged Brigitte, the woman who found Anna's lifeless body in that Florida hotel room. "We didn't judge her. I didn't know anything about her. Mr. Nygard said I met her once at his house, but I don't remember. There are always beautiful women there. I never heard of her, as I don't go tabloid. But of course I was curious to meet her and when I met her . . . I just welcomed her. This is what we do."

"I think the courtesy we extended to her, she appreciated," King Eric said. "I don't use the word 'abuse,' but I think some kind of things had happened to her where she didn't trust anybody. And she put a lot of trust into my family. She'd go away and leave Mrs. Gibson alone with the baby . . . so that's a lot of trust. She just mistrusts everybody."

"I was told she was looking for someone to do some babysitting," Mrs. Gibson told me. Mrs. Gibson is the woman who was caring for Dannielynn when Anna Nicole Smith took her last breath. "She did have a nanny that come from away. It was time for the nanny to leave.

"I was asked if I could fill in for the nanny, and I thought it a good idea to go meet Anna," Mrs. Gibson continued. "We spoke for a while, exchanged some words. I asked her if she believed in God." Both Quethlie Alexis and Nadine Alexie said that they too had conversations with Anna about God, often reading the Bible to her.

The nannies, who say they are now scared for their lives and are afraid of being deported, said in an interview on *Controversy TV*, "She's a nice person, a lovely person, someone you know you feel good to be around."

The first time Mrs. Gibson met Anna she asked her, "Would you like me to pray with you?" Anna had answered yes.

"Everyone who was in her room at the time, we all held hands and prayed."

During the first conversation with Mrs. Gibson, Anna said, "I wish you were my nanny."

"No doubt, something could work out," Mrs. Gibson said with a smile. "I'll be more than happy to assist in whatever way that I can."

And that's how her twelve-dollar an hour babysitting job with Anna Nicole Smith began.

Mrs. Gibson never had a problem being paid.

• • •

Everyone I interviewed who knew Anna during her short life in the Bahamas described her similarly: she was a very sweet person in very dark times. And they described her patterns and habits similarly as well, much of which included a lot of sleep and a lot of drugs.

"I tried to get her out of the house," King Eric told me. "I think she stays in the house too much. She's a little fragile. When she thinks too much she get into tears. She never understand why her son had to die. She never understand that. So the thing to do is not to let her think, so keep her occupied and then she's happy."

"I believe in nature and the healing powers of nature," Brigitte recounted. "I wanted her to get out more and have some more kind of spirituality that would help her . . . . I wanted to sort of draw her away and get her away from all her troubles, get her on a different track."

Then there was Dannielynn. Brigitte would speak only her native German with Dannielynn. The baby found it humorous, perhaps because everyone else found it silly. "It's good for babies to do that and everyone thought it was so funny,"

Brigitte laughed. Singing the baby little German songs when they were together had an added benefit. It made Anna lighten up. "I don't like to go back and brood," Brigitte said. "I'm the opposite and get over it."

Like Brigitte and King Eric, his ex-wife, Mrs. Gibson, also felt an extreme closeness with Anna, and attempted to help her feel better about her days. "Anna Nicole called me 'Mommy,'" Mrs. Gibson told me proudly. "One day I was standing in her living room and she put her arm around me and she hugged me."

"You're all the Mommy that I have," Anna said so sweetly. "I wish I had a family like yours."

Mrs. Gibson says she saw a broken person. "Very sad," Mrs. Gibson remembers. "When she smiled, I always complimented her because I so seldom saw her smile. 'I'm glad to see my girl smiling today.' I called her 'my girl.'" Mrs. Gibson said that Anna cried often, saying her son's death was so difficult to handle. "She'd lie in her bed and sob and sob and sob. She would sometimes say, 'I want to go where Daniel is' and question, 'Why did God take Daniel? I wish it was me instead.'"

One particular day, Anna was wailing in her bedroom and Mrs. Gibson went to check on what was wrong with Anna. When she went into her room, Anna was on her back on the bed. She had a big poster-size photo of Daniel covering part of her body. "The picture part was down on her face," Mrs. Gibson told me.

Anna Nicole Smith was looking at that photo of her dead son and crying.

Anna would spend most of her days in bed, surrounded by her four dogs: Sugar Pie, a poodle; Marilyn, a white silky terrier named after her idol; Puppy, a shih tzu; and another shih tzu that seemed to be nameless. She'd sleep, wake up, play with the dogs, take some drugs, then go back to sleep. She wouldn't do much else. "Physically she was okay," Mrs. Gibson said. "But emotionally she was stressed out. Too stressed. That's all I can say."

The nannies say that Howard was cold, never helping Anna whenever she fell out of bed or near the pool. Moe, Anna's bodyguard, also told private investigators that one day Anna fell into the pool and Howard yelled at him, "Anna's at the bottom of the pool. Howard was just standing there and I had to jump in."

Moe has said that Anna fired Howard and Moe several times while in the Bahamas, but they always talked her into hiring them back. Moe says he convinced Anna several times to keep Howard and he now feels guilty knowing Anna died with so many drugs in her system.

The nannies both have said that Anna often slept for more than twenty-four hours straight, often so "drugged out" that she would stay in bed for days. Two days down, one day up, two days down. It was a depressing cycle.

One of the nannies, Nadine Alexie, had gone to pharmacology school for a year, so she knew a little about prescription drugs. According to their statements, when Anna's psychiatrist, Dr. Khris, would visit from Los Angeles, she'd say Anna needed lots of medicine. Dr. Khris would arrange the medicine in little cups, and line them up. Every four hours like clockwork, Howard would take a cup and go to Anna's bedroom. He'd wake her up and give her the medicine. Howard, they say, was always the one to give Anna her drugs.

The little cups were packed with medicine, often six to ten pills at a time. Nadine said she got scared that with that much medicine being taken, if something were to happen to Anna that people around the house, like the lower level employees, would get blamed for it. So, Nadine kept a list of what Howard was giving Anna. A religious woman, Nadine swore before God as her witness that what she says is true.

According to the nanny's carefully kept notes, Anna was taking a staggering twenty-four drugs at one time. The drugs were kept all over the house: in Anna's refrigerator, the guest bathroom cabinet, and in the guest room. She says the photograph released by the website TMZ, showing Anna's refrigerator filled with methadone, B-complex, vitamin B-12, and Slimfast, was real, not staged as Howard's team has suggested.

After Daniel died neither Anna nor Howard felt like eating, so Dr. Khris recommended Slimfast as a substitute food to keep them going. Howard didn't eat much at all, the nannies say, he just smoked constantly and nervously.

"When she'd fall, Howard wouldn't pick her up," Nadine noted. "But Howard didn't miss a beat when giving her those drugs."

Mrs. Gibson was gentler in her thoughts about Howard. "I thought it would be remiss of me if I did not compliment Howard on the care he was taking for Anna," Mrs. Gibson told me. "He would get up in the night and fix her whatever she needed. He would see to it she got whatever she needs. He would see to it that she gets it, which in my opinion wasn't too much."

"Friends don't let other friends drive drunk," fashion mogul and former Anna boyfriend, Peter Nygard, told me. "In Howard's case, he gave her the car keys. He was irresponsible in the way he acted, calling himself her custodian, but not taking care of her as he should. He eliminated everyone in her life." Peter says Howard was probably happy to keep her so intoxicated because she needed him more. "It seems he enjoyed the fact she was so out of it. I don't think she'd be dead today if she was under my watch."

Jackie Hatten, Anna's friend and godmother of Daniel, flew to the Bahamas for two days in October to "save Anna." After Daniel's death, Jackie feared that Anna was next. Jackie stayed with Peter Nygard, who confirms Anna and Jackie were good friends and that Jackie also lived with Anna.

Anna dated Jackie's brother, Mark. That relationship ended in his arrest and imprisonment. Hatten, an artist, served a seven-year sentence for making "terrorist threats" against Anna and blames Howard K. Stern for his imprisonment. Hatten claims that it was all a setup by Howard K. Stern, who, he says, called police and told them Anna had a stalker that was on his way to his house with a gun. Jackie said that her brother and Anna had just had a big fight and he was coming over to pack up his stuff since they had been living together. When I spoke to Mark Hatten from prison in the spring of 2007, he told me, "Howard wanted me out of Anna's life, he was jealous that we were close. He did this to silence me."

Law enforcement sources confirmed that in June 2000, the FBI interviewed Hatten in prison. He claimed Anna Nicole and Howard K. Stern wanted him to arrange a hit on Pierce Marshall, J. Howard Marshall's son and their bitter rival in the war for her late husband's money. The FBI asked him to wear a wire and secretly tape Anna Nicole, which he later refused to do. Hatten told me on the phone from prison that he still loved her and didn't want to see her get sent to prison. He also claims that Howard once gave him two small pills, saying they were aspirin. Hatten says the pills knocked him out, and he was unconscious for at least twenty-four hours.

His younger sister Jackie believes this was just another example of Howard K. Stern manipulating Anna's life. "Jackie's probably right based on what I saw myself," Peter Nygard told me. "Howard cut everyone else out of Anna's life, especially those that tried to help her."

Peter experienced this himself. "She called me several times when she got to the Bahamas, often leaving a message," Peter said. "I would call her back, and Howard always picked up the phone. She never got the messages, because she never called back after each time. One time when she phoned me again, I asked, 'why didn't you call me back?'"

"I never got your message!" she said.

"One time she called my house asking if we could have dinner. I called back and Howard answered the phone. I offered that she could come over to my house for dinner, and Howard responded like a jealous boyfriend. I know she never got the message."

• • •

When Jackie arrived in the Bahamas on her mission to save Anna in October 2006, she tried to call Anna a few times from Peter Nygard's house. But whoever answered the phone, always hung up. Persistent, Jackie went over to Anna's house. When she got there, she realized she couldn't just go up to the door and knock as the security was tight at the fortress-like home. Jackie announced her presence on the intercom at the locked gate. "Anna's not in any shape for visitors," she heard Howard say in the background. Then, someone promptly told her to leave the premises immediately. She believes Howard didn't want her to see how drugged Anna was.

"She told them she was staying at my place," Peter said. "After Jackie told me what happened, I told her she might as well take off and go back home. So she left. Then, Anna called me either that same night or the next night asking where Jackie was."

"I wanted to see her," Anna said. Peter explained that Jackie had been turned away at the gate. "Is she still there?" Anna asked. "I'd love to talk to her."

"It sounded like she absolutely would've seen Jackie if she could've," Peter told me. "She sounded sincere. I told Jackie about it, but Jackie could never get through to her again."

Jackie told Peter that Anna was in imminent danger. She felt Howard was increasingly drugging her so he could inherit the money. She said someone needed to save Anna's life to "take her away from Howard."

"He may try to kill her," Jackie said. "Howard is responsible for killing the boy and Anna's next."

"I thought at the time they were wild claims," Peter said. "But sure enough Anna is dead a few months later."

When I asked King Eric and Brigitte whether or not they had seen any drugs or prescription medications in the house, Brigitte said, "I didn't look for it. If it was hidden someplace, then, I mean, you don't rummage through people's things."

"Howard Stern doesn't push anything on Anna," King Eric quickly interjected. "Trust me, nobody push nothing on Anna. Whatever she does, she wanna do it. I don't care how it look to you, she doesn't do anything nobody want. Matter of fact, if you wanted her to do something, tell her NOT to do it. If you want her not to do it, tell her TO do it. That's how bad she is like that."

"Howard wasn't controlling," Mrs. Gibson, the babysitter, told me. "I have never seen that of him. He was the quietest man going." Then, without my asking another question, she added an unexpected postscript, "He didn't seem like he was after the money."

• • •

Anna's mother Virgie Arthur also felt that Howard K. Stern was after Anna's money and went on television to say so. "She's the one making the money," she said in an interview aired on *Entertainment Tonight*. "And the people surrounding her are gaining from it, so they don't want any of the family around. I don't know why they don't want the family around. We have never asked for anything. She has never given us anything."

Virgie was devastated that she was not invited to the funeral of her grandson, Daniel, whom she raised until he was around six-years-old. She also told me she tried to contact Anna numerous times, but each time she was either hung up on or the phone number had been changed.

A week before Daniel's funeral, Virgie went on CNN and said, "I know that Danny had a trust fund [claiming Anna's former husband, billionaire J. Howard Marshall, set one up for him]. . . . But if Howard marries Vickie and Daniel's gone, that leaves Howard and the baby to inherit whatever money she has." And then she made her point even clearer. "If Howard Stern marries her and she ends up dead, then who does the money go to?" Howard K. Stern.

Before ending the interview, Virgie Arthur pleaded, "Vickie Lynn, you know I love you, always have." Then, she looked right in the camera and added, "And be careful about who you hang around with, because you may be next."

November

After her mother's attention-getting interview on CNN, Anna Nicole made sure her first television interview since the death of her son was blockbuster. Heavily promoted by *Entertainment Tonight*, the "most riveting interview you have ever seen" would be stretched out over an entire November ratings sweeps week and would include everything from a rant against her mother to graphic video Howard K. Stern had taken of Anna's c-section delivery of Dannielynn.

Before the airdate, reporter Mark Steines, who was invited to Horizons for the interview, said that fear of the paparazzi had turned Anna into a veritable recluse. In a blog on the *Entertainment Tonight* Web site, he wrote: "There are absolutely no signs of life on the outside. I would come to learn that the fear of constant paparazzi keeps Anna and her support team locked up, blinds drawn, and constantly aware that prying eyes are trying to snap photos.

"There is a pool no one uses, gardens no one visits and terraces no one stands on to take in the warm night air. Anna and her baby live pretty much like prisoners inside this home."

Steines also noted that Anna Nicole seemed like a changed person, nothing like the bubbly, childlike blonde he'd interviewed in the past. "She's calmer, sadder, a bit of a broken bird, yet she looked quite beautiful."

The "world exclusive" interview only increased the maelstrom that had become Anna Nicole Smith's life. Tongues wagged that Anna, with a new trendy haircut, seemed highly sedated and was slurring her words. When asked about this interview later in Judge Seidlin's courtroom, Howard K. Stern would say that he'd seen her "more impaired than that." Judge Seidlin was stunned and thought the statement shocking, leading some legal commentators to later call it Howard's "Freudian slip."

During the interview, Howard K. Stern sat next to her, looking uncomfortable and awkward, seeming unsure of what she would say next. She giggled when she talked about the first time she realized she was in love with Howard. She beamed "like a mother" Steines said, when she held Dannielynn and asked the seven-week-old, "Can you say Mommy?"

When she mentioned her son, Daniel, she began sobbing. "Daniel's dead! Daniel's dead!" she cried. "This was not supposed to happen." With tears streaming down her face, she wondered, "I don't understand why God took him and didn't take me."

Then, she turned her anger and venom toward her mother. Furious that Virgie had gone on CNN and "said I killed my son or Howard killed my son," Anna huffed that Virgie was only her birth mother, "not my real mother." Anna asked, "Who does she think she is" to go out and make "ridiculous statements about me killing my son?"

For the record, according to the CNN transcript, Virgie Arthur never accused Anna of killing her son.

"She didn't know him, she didn't know me," Anna explained bitterly. "She never really wanted to know me because she was too jealous of me . . . . I saw how evil she was and evil she looked. So, bring it on Mom, Mommie Dearest. Bring it on!"

The following week when *Entertainment Tonight* was showing Howard K. Stern's "beautiful" and "uncensored" home video of a screaming, heavily medicated Anna Nicole in the hospital having a c-section delivery of Dannielynn, Anna Nicole Smith was back in the same Bahamian hospital. This time she had pneumonia.

• • •

"She didn't seem good," her new friend King Eric remembers. "I took her when she was sick and needed to go to the doctor.

Howard couldn't get her to go to the doctor. Howard had to call me." When King Eric got to Horizons, he found a very sick Anna Nicole in bed, obviously sedated, and complaining that her back hurt.

"Listen Anna," King Eric told her. "This is Daddy. Daddy say you have to go to the doctor and that's where you gotta go. I'm gonna call and I will make a reservation and I'm gonna take you personally."

Anna put on her childish voice and asked, "Will you do that?"

"Yes," King Eric promised. "I will do that."

At first he took her to a chiropractor because she was complaining of intense back pain. The chiropractor said it wasn't her back. He told them that Anna needed to be seen by a physician. So, King Eric took her to a local walk-in clinic, and the doctor at the clinic said they needed to take her to the hospital, "*Now.*"

Anna immediately said, "No way!"

And King Eric responded, "Daddy say you gotta go. Daddy's gonna take you. Daddy and Howard are gonna stay and be with you all the time."

"Okay," she relinquished. "Then, I will go. If you're going to be there, I will go."

Anna Nicole had a very bad case of pneumonia and doctors quickly got her on oxygen, antibiotics, and monitors. Then, they drained fluid from her lungs. It was "very serious," doctors said. She was in the hospital for six days.

• • •

Throughout the next three months, Brigitte and Mrs. Gibson—Anna's two "mommies"—would call the house to check in on

Anna and drop by for visits. Brigitte said that she would call and Howard would say, "She's under the weather" or "She has an upset stomach" or "It might be the flu."

"She became more to me like a daughter," babysitter Mrs. Gibson said. "I would call and check on her. Most of the time, he would answer the phone. I would ask how she was doing today. He'd say she 'wasn't doing good' or sometimes she'd be 'pretty good.'"

On November 14, less than a week after she was out of the hospital, Anna felt good enough to go look at a new house. It was a full two weeks after she was supposed to have already moved out of the Horizons house, as ordered by Ben Thompson's hand-delivered notice to vacate the premises as she had not yet paid the mortgage. She and all of her belongings had not budged, but she was looking at other real estate options.

Gregg White, a broker with King's Real Estate, was showing her his own house, a 5000 square foot lakeside home with one and a half acres of water frontage in central Nassau. The asking price was $1.89 million. Howard had already previewed the house and liked it, so Anna decided to go look at it for herself. When she had looked at houses on an episode of E! Entertainment's *The Anna Nicole Show*, she had flopped around on the beds, climbed in the tubs and pretended to bathe, and talked about sex a lot. This adventure didn't seem too far afield.

Her driver took her to the luxury lakefront house where she met broker Gregg White. She was wearing a loose, baggy sweat suit and slippers. She was, as Gregg remembers, "strikingly beautiful, very tall." She was, however, noticeably "very clumsy" and was "dragging her feet." Gregg says she kept stumbling "and almost tripped over the Oriental rug in the house." And "her speech was slurred and slow."

There had been lots of stories in the Bahamian press around the time about the problems they were having with the Horizons house and their permanent residency. "It was obvious they were scrambling to do an actual investment," Gregg told me. "I definitely got the sense from Howard that there was a sense of urgency so he could meet the requirement."

Anna was quite flirtatious during her tour with Gregg, grabbing his arm and getting close to him. "She definitely tries to flirt her way into your favor," he remembers, "batting her eyes and showing off her pearly white teeth." Gregg told her, "I'd rather keep it straight business."

When he showed her the big game room downstairs, she talked about her stripping days saying, "I'm going to put a dancer's pole in this room. You know I started out like that, and I need to practice again." Gregg laughed, but kept the tour moving.

Anna decided the house—its marble floors, spacious bathrooms, and waterfront setting—would work for her. So, she moved to make her pitch. "She acted as though she didn't have any money," Gregg said, "and tried to structure an IOU deal." This made Gregg White incredibly uncomfortable. "She wanted to wait to make payments till the end of November, saying she had a lot of money coming in then from a TV deal, since it was 'sweeps week,' and then she'd have more coming from a film deal later."

Gregg White was not interested in an IOU from Anna Nicole Smith. "It was just weird," he remembers. "From a business standpoint there was a lot to be suspicious about. But you could see she loved life and was charming."

December

King Eric had first met Anna through her friend Peter Nygard in 2000 at one of his famous parties. He was introduced to her again when she moved to the Bahamas after she met his son, Shane Gibson, the Bahamian Immigration Minister. King Eric was known around town as the guy who took lots of VIPs out on his boat. He was used to celebrities. King Eric and Brigitte started taking Anna out on the waters.

"I cooked her a meal on the boat and she loved it," King Eric remembers. "She said, 'You could come to my house sometime and cook a meal.' I said, 'Anytime, Anna. Anytime.'"

Late in the year, Brigitte and Eric, Anna's "Mommy" and "Daddy," began coming over more often to cook for Anna. Sometimes twice a week. "Matter of fact," King Eric said, "the only time she eat a real meal is when I cook. She loved Bahamian, loved fried fish Bahamian style. She was really adorable."

"I do knitting and a lot of crafts," Brigitte told me. "And when we'd wait for the fish to boil, I would knit."

"I wish I could knit," Anna commented, watching Brigitte's hands play with the yarn.

"It's not hard to learn," Brigitte told her, showing how she used the needles to hook the yarn into tight knots. Brigitte told Anna that when someone has a baby it is a tradition that somebody knits something for the baby.

"Dannielynn didn't get anything," Anna had said.

"So, I decided to make her a blanket for Dannielynn," Brigitte told me. "And I brought it over there at Christmas and she was very gracious and she was just really touched."

"Thank you so much, Mommy," Anna told Brigitte through tears.

"Not at all . . . " Brigitte smiled.

• • •

Peter Nygard spoke to Anna for the last time shortly before Christmas. They had talked about getting together for dinner and Anna wanted to know if he was going to have his annual big New Year's Eve party. "I told her I was not, that I was going to Miami for New Year's," he said. "I wish I saw her. I could've saved her. Each of her last calls seemed like she was almost reaching out for help."

"Christmas is always an emotional kind of holiday," Brigitte reminisced.

"We attend church, we all attend church," King Eric said. That December, Anna went with them. King Eric was in the choir and they were playing music with the choir singing.

It was in this "tiny little chapel," as Brigitte described it. "It was so beautiful and then the violinist began playing on the violin and it gave you goose bumps."

King Eric began singing "Amazing Grace."

Anna began crying as King Eric sang the lyrics from the choir: "Amazing grace, how sweet the sound that saved a wretch like me! I once was lost, but now am found, Was blind, but now I see." While on the "trail of tears," it is said the Cherokee Indians were not always able to give their dead a full and proper burial. So, instead, the singing of "Amazing Grace" in their native tongue had to suffice.

By the time this verse came: "Through many dangers, toils and snares, I have already come; 'Tis grace has brought me safe thus far, And grace will lead me home," Anna had rushed down the aisle and was sobbing outside the back of the church.

"I couldn't figure out why she walked out," King Eric said. Then, he realized it was the same song sung at Daniel's funeral.

January

By January, despite continuing to fight with Ben Thompson over payments toward Horizons and not being able to pay some employees, Anna had been able to buy a house and now was buying a boat. Both of which, King Eric was to help her with—the first, helping to oversee the renovations at the house, and, the second, as her captain, getting the boat from Florida to the Bahamas. It remains a mystery where the money came from to make these expensive purchases.

Anna also made her first high-profile public appearance since her son's death. She joined a sell-out crowd of 5,238 at the Hard Rock Hotel in Hollywood, Florida, to watch the man they call "Tremendous" live up to his nickname. After a two-year layoff, "Tremendous," left-hander Travis Simms, reclaimed his boxing super welterweight title with a ninth-round technical knockout.

About his glitterati crowd, promoter Don King crowed, "I'm bringing Hollywood to Hollywood." Anna seemed to enjoy watching the fight from her ringside seat—along with other notables such as Hulk Hogan, Rev. Al Sharpton, and rapper Fat Joe—as Simms delivered punishing blows to the head and body of his opponent Jose Antonio Rivera.

After the fight, Simms announced, "I'm back. I did what I had to do . . . it was just a matter of time." Anna was back too, showing her smile, taking pictures, and waving to her well-wishing fans. She also showed off her new tattoo to Hulk

Hogan. The photos of her experience would be the last public photographs ever taken of the model. A month later she would be dead.

February 5, 2007

Anna was excited. After having her morning injection into her left buttock, she headed for a ten o'clock dance lesson for a music video she was producing for an upcoming TrimSpa event. Around 11:00 a.m., after she got home from her rehearsal, she called Mrs. Gibson.

"Mommy?" Anna asked. "We want to go to Florida today to bring the boat back. Can you take care of Dannielynn until we get back?"

"What time do you want me to come?" Mrs. Gibson replied.

"Now, if you can," Anna said.

"I can be there around one o'clock," Mrs. Gibson told her. Mrs. Gibson got all her errands done and rushed over to Horizons. When she arrived, she learned that the flight had been delayed. It would now leave at 4:30 p.m. Anna spent the rest of her time playing with Dannielynn. She was kissing her from head to foot, making her laugh. The baby giggled, and smiled ear to ear.

When it was time to leave, Anna turned to Mrs. Gibson and said, "Now you pray for me."

"I'm always praying for you, Anna," Mrs. Gibson said.

Then Anna went over and hugged Mrs. Gibson. "That was a different kind of hug," Mrs. Gibson remembers. "She hugged me like she didn't want to let me go." Howard announced that

they had to go or they'd miss their flight. Mrs. Gibson won-
ders now if Anna felt something, if she had a premonition.

"I do have a little belief in destiny," King Eric told me.
"Things happen that you don't know is gonna happen, but all
the signs are there and you never really think about it until it
happens. And then you think, geez, it was right in front of my
eyes all the time, but I just didn't see it."

Before she walked out the door, Anna turned and told Mrs.
Gibson, "I want you to take care of Dannielynn. I know she's
in good hands."

CHAPTER 7

Breaking News

3:48 p.m. EST
MSNBC Television
Breaking News

RITA COSBY: I understand we have Ron Rale now with
us exclusively on the phone. Ron, you and I just
spoke a few moments ago off camera, tell us what
you know.

RON RALE: I can confirm that Anna Nicole is deceased.
I don't have the cause right now, obviously there's
going to be an autopsy. I was informed by a gentleman who was in the room with Howard Stern, who
is obviously speechless as all of us are. But they
want me to address this so . . . nobody there is able
to talk, so I'm giving you the information. I don't
have anything more right now. Anna did have some

flu symptoms. I believe the last couple of days she wasn't feeling well, I think she had a fever. But, it's just shocking. And, I don't know anything more right now. I'm trying to find out, just like you guys are. But it is confirmed that she has passed away.

RITA COSBY: How did you find out the news?

RON RALE: I was trying to find out with the help of the media, the backlines to the hospital. But I actually got a call from Howard Stern's cell phone, and it was another gentleman, Howard was unable to speak, but they gave me the information.

RITA COSBY: Have you talked to the family at all?

RON RALE: I haven't spoke to anybody. This is all just news to me. We're gonna find out . . . it's unbelievable. I almost still didn't believe it. I'm having a hard time believing it, but that is what I'm informed. Howard was in the background there I think, but it's . . . this is just a horrible, horrible thing. I'll let you know more when I find out more.

RITA COSBY: Give a sense of some of the pressure, you and I were talking earlier, just about the pressure that's been on her mentally, physically in the last few months.

RON RALE: I have been concerned because I don't think anybody should have to endure what she's endured, having lost her son and people attacking her left and right. And frankly I don't want to get emotional or angry about this right now, but I don't know what the cause was . . . . It's just I felt like Anna was the underdog having all of this thrust upon her and she really just wanted to be a mom and she was a good mom, and this is uh, tragic.

On February 8, 2007, at 3:48 p.m., I broke the story on MSNBC, getting the official word that Anna Nicole Smith had died. Details of her death spread quickly, completely overshadowing all other news stories. Though there were other, more urgent world events—including a sixth chopper downed in Iraq in three weeks, and the death of our nation's troops—the death of Anna Nicole Smith, TrimSpa spokesperson extraordinaire, received unparalleled coverage. The day of her death, NBC's Nightly News devoted fourteen seconds to Iraq compared to three minutes and thirty seconds to Anna Nicole; more than ten percent of its entire newscast focused on the death of the blonde model. That night, NBC's cable network, MSNBC, aired more than three solid hours of coverage strictly devoted to her death.

In short, America was riveted by this story. Here's how it went:

LARRY KING: The death of Anna Nicole Smith—it's the number one story around the world tonight.

BILL O'REILLY: Thank you for watching us tonight. The talking points memo will be in our second segment this evening . . . . First, 39-year old Anna Nicole Smith dead in Florida.

JOE SCARBOROUGH: For better or for worse, would you call Anna Nicole Smith an American icon of the early 21st Century?

The story had really caught fire around 2:45 pm, when our newsroom at MSNBC, like other newsrooms around the country, had sparked with the news that Anna Nicole had collapsed at the Hard Rock Hotel in Florida. I had just finished my shift, but the managing producer asked if I would come back into the studio to talk to the public about what I knew about Anna—from her wild past to her crazy present and its cast of high-rolling eccentric characters. Over the last several months, I had become acquainted with many in the Anna Nicole circle, including doing an attention-getting exclusive interview with Larry Birkhead.

I was already aware of some behind-the-scenes legal dramas in the case, as well as many of the current pressures Anna Nicole was under. In late September 2006, during a lengthy, late night conversation, a distraught Larry Birkhead revealed to me yet untold specific and jaw dropping details of his relationship with Anna Nicole. He also presented what he believed was clear proof of his being the father of her baby. I was quite surprised by the amount of evidence and dates he had collected to build his case, and was impressed by how passionate this then unknown photographer was that Howard K. Stern was putting on a huge hoax to the American public, since Howard had just gone on *Larry King* announcing he was the father to the world. Larry Birkhead described Howard as being an enormous con artist and liar, someone who deeply facilitated Anna Nicole's drug habit.

As our discussion continued that evening, Larry asked me, as he told me he had done with several other journalists, if I had any recommendations for a "pit bull" lawyer who would essentially have the wherewithal to stand up to the spin machine of Howard K. Stern. He knew he was in the middle of a David and Goliath fight.

I suggested a few names, including Debra Opri whom I knew from her representation of the Michael Jackson family during his contentious child molestation case. Larry asked if I would call her and make the introduction. At that time, Opri didn't know anything about the story, and after I explained some details, she said, "If this is true, he should be declared the father and see his child. This is explosive."

I learned days later, they had met and reached an agreement amongst themselves on representation. I was not aware of the specific details or arrangements. My job was to cover the story.

Months later, minutes after the news broke that Anna Nicole Smith had been rushed to the hospital, I was trying to put truth to the rumors already being churned by the gossip mill—various sources claimed that she was everything from drunk to drugged. Was it just another kooky episode for this reality TV star or was there more?

I immediately called Anna's attorney, Ron Rale, to ask him about her condition. Since Ron had often spoken on Anna's behalf in the on-going paternity suit, and was a long time friend of Howard K. Stern's, I knew he would be one of the few people who could get immediate access to information about her health. "We've heard she collapsed," I said after momentary pleasantries. "But do you know any more?"

At 3:38 p.m. EST, I was on the air. I had just finished speaking with Ron Rale, Anna's attorney, who had just gotten word that she had collapsed. He said that he had heard in the last few days that she was not feeling well and had flu like symptoms. She had been woozy, nauseous. His reaction to the latest news: he was frantic. He was calling the hospital and getting more details. He said he hadn't gotten any calls or talked to the hospital yet. I asked if he'd mind calling the hospital again and getting an update on her condition. I told him I'd call back in ten minutes.

None of us could have imagined the tragic turn of events that Anna Nicole's weird world had suddenly taken. When I got Ron on the phone again, he was notably somber. "Rita," he said, pausing. "She's deceased."

"Deceased?" I repeated.

"She's dead, Rita," Ron said, with bewilderment. "Dead."

"Are you sure?" I asked.

He was. He'd heard it from the hospital and confirmed it with someone in the room with Howard K. Stern, explaining that Howard was too distraught to speak to him personally. Without hesitation, I asked what any reporter would have in the situation: "Will you go on the air with that terrible news?"

At first he said no. Then, he said he would in an hour. I told him it was important for people to hear the news first from someone who cared so deeply about Anna. "Would you do it right now?" I asked. Thirty seconds later, after he had composed himself, Ron Rale told the world: "Anna Nicole is deceased."

● ● ●

My afternoon on-air session was non-stop. I connected with sources and friends of Anna Nicole's during commercial breaks and then went live with them moments later. In the four o'clock hour I talked to David Granoff, Anna's former publicist and close friend to her for ten years. He told me he was "very sad, but not shocked." Remembering that Anna was always in and out of the hospital with so many terrible things happening in her life. He said when he saw her on TV recently that he thought there was no spark anymore. "I kind of had this in the back of my mind that something like this was going to happen." Then, he asked, "What was she found with? A mixture of drugs or something?"

Just after 4:30 p.m. EST, Seminole Police Chief Charlie Tiger held a press conference and said, "All I know is the nurse called at 1:38 p.m., called the hotel operator . . . . Only the nurse was in the room at the time." When a question was raised from the throng of reporters about where the bodyguard was, he answered, "He came in at a later time to administer CPR."

Around 5:15 pm. EST on MSNBC, Captain Dan Fitzgerald from Hollywood Fire and Rescue said in a taped interview with WTVJ that Anna Nicole Smith was found "unconscious and not breathing." He said there is no way of knowing how long she'd been down before she was discovered.

At the top of the six o'clock hour, I was talking live on the air with Peter Nygard. He said he had known her for ten years, dated her for three, and that they still remained close. "Anna Nicole kept telling me years ago she had a death wish," Peter announced, "that she pictured herself like a Marilyn Monroe and she would die the same way as Marilyn Monroe would, and all of a sudden here we are."

Around the same time, Alex Goen, the CEO and founder of TrimSpa released to the press a written statement: "Today Anna Nicole Smith's grief stricken and tumultuous personal life came to an end. Anna came to our company as a customer, but she departs it as a friend. While life for Anna Nicole was not easy these past few months, she held dear her husband Howard K. Stern, her daughter Dannielynn Hope, her most cherished friends, beloved dogs and finally her work with TrimSpa . . . Anna knew both the joy of giving life and the heartache of losing a child. We pray that she is granted the peace that eluded her more recent days on earth and that she finds comfort in the presence of her son, Daniel."

Minutes after the statement was released, *Extra* correspondent Carlos Diaz highlighted on MSNBC that it seemed apparent to him that Alex Goen and his diet pill company, TrimSpa, were immediately trying to take a step away from Anna Nicole. "If you listen to the wording in that statement," Carlos reported, "TrimSpa is saying Anna Nicole Smith 'came to us as a customer.' That to me is very, very gutsy to say it in that way because basically they're already distancing themselves from Anna Nicole saying in essence she's not a spokesperson, she's not an employee, you know, because of the class action lawsuit that's being filed. She came to us as a customer. That to me says, you know, kind of good riddance to Anna Nicole. I find that to be very telling on TrimSpa's part."

Earlier that week, Anna Nicole Smith and TrimSpa, Inc. had been named in a class action lawsuit alleging their marketing of a weight-loss pill was false and misleading to consumers as well as "deceptive business practices."

Prior to her death, Alex Goen had already decided that Anna was going to be moved aside by a new face. Alex Goen told *Access Hollywood* that Anna "recognized her story was getting old and we needed some fresh stories."

"So, she was already going to step down?" correspondent Tim Vincent asked.

"I wouldn't call it step down," Goen responded. "She was going to share the throne."

CHAPTER 8

The Anna Nicole Show

THE DAY SHE DIED EVERYONE TOLD THEIR STORY OF THE SPECIAL "it" girl from the Lone Star State, with the curvaceous body who became famous for being famous.

Anna Nicole Smith was born Vickie Lynn Hogan on November 28, 1967, in Mexia, Texas, a town of little more than five square miles about forty miles east of Waco. The town's motto? "A great place, no matter how you pronounce it." Her childhood was fair to middling. Her mother had a steady job as a sheriff's deputy, if not a steady husband. Virgie had Vickie when she was just sixteen years old, and told me that Don Hogan, Vickie's real father, was abusive. He beat Virgie so bad when she was pregnant with Vickie that Virgie would lay on the floor and crawl in a circle so that the baby would be protected and wouldn't get punched.

"He did rape my ten-year-old sister and her young friend at the same time when I was married to him," Virgie said. "He was charged and served sixty days in jail and five years probation." He moved out the day that Virgie says she finally fought back after all the abuse. She threw a ketchup bottle at him. He left and never came back. Three weeks before Vickie's second birthday, they were officially divorced.

Anna ended up with several half siblings, through her mother's and father's marriages, including three half brothers and two half sisters. Her younger half brother, Donnie Hogan, lived with their father in Texas until he was old enough to work. He says their father abused him both physically and emotionally, including making him witness the killing of a neighbor's dog. "He was an alcoholic and worse when he was sober," Donnie told me. "If I hate anyone on this earth, it would be him."

Donnie, now the father of two twin boys, said that his and Vickie's dad was a devil worshipper and even has a tattoo of a devil with a pitchfork on his arm. "I'd catch him praying to Satan, and saying, 'I have the power of the devil,'" Donnie remembers. The last time he saw his father "he took out a gun and was praying to Satan . . . Dad put a gun to his mouth, to his head, and to others' heads. And then he put a gun to my head."

After Anna Nicole had become a nationally recognized beauty, Donnie says the two of them cried at least twice together about the abuse they both endured. She told him that she had been physically abused, and claimed her real father and her stepfather molested her. The abuse affected her. "She could never trust anybody," Donnie said

Virgie says that she does not believe the stepfather ever molested Vickie, but does not know if Vickie's real dad ever did anything to her when Vickie and her father reunited many years later after Virgie's divorce.

Virgie says she did discipline her daughter, occasionally

using a wide, thick leather belt to discipline her. She gave her the last "ass whooping" when Vickie was sixteen. "She didn't come home from school," Virgie remembers, "and I finally found her at a friend's house at 3 a.m. I brought her home and told her to 'bend it over.' And then I whooped her butt."

Virgie says that otherwise Anna had a decent life, and thinks that Vickie created the "poor pitiful me story" because she thought it "worked better," that rags to riches was a much better story to sell to the media.

After failing her freshman year of high school, Vickie Lynn dropped out, and began working at Jim's Krispy Fried Chicken. In 1984, at the age of 17, she married a co-worker, a fry cook named Billy Smith. They had a son that same year. Virgie picked the name "Daniel"—"Like Daniel in the Bible," she said.

But Virgie didn't get to name her own daughter. She told me that the woman who would become "Anna Nicole Smith" was supposed to be named "Kathleen Kay." Virgie says she loved that name and had decided on it before the baby was born. When she went into labor, her husband wasn't around, so her own mother went with her to the hospital. While Virgie was asleep her mother filled out the birth certificate. "When I woke up," Virgie remembers, "my mother said, 'I didn't name her what she's supposed to be. I named her after you.'"

"Virgie?" Virgie asked.

"No, no," her mother said. "You know how people mess up on your name and call you 'Vickie'? I named her Vickie and I thought it should be 'Vickie Lynn.' I like the way it sounded."

So, seventeen years later, Vickie Lynn Hogan became Vickie Lynn Smith, mother to Daniel Wayne Smith, wife of Billy. The marriage, however, to Billy Smith didn't go well. They separated shortly after Daniel's birth. Around this time, Vickie was jumping from job to job, including stints at Wal-Mart and Red Lobster. One day, desperate to make more money to help support herself and young Daniel, she followed a sign to her destiny. She said she spotted a "neon lady" on a glowing sign "in high-heel shoes and she had a bikini on and it would flash tiptoe and back, tiptoe and back." It was a sign for a Houston "gentleman's club."

Her mother Virgie, the sheriff's deputy, thought Vickie was still working at the Red Lobster until Vickie's boyfriend one day told her that she was now stripping. Virgie decided she'd go see for herself. She parked her patrol car right in front of the strip club and marched inside. Her law enforcement uniform drew almost as much attention as her daughter, who was gyrating in "nothing but a g-string" right in front of "some old man's face."

Seeing a uniformed officer, the manager rushed over to see if there were any problems. "Do you see that woman who's butt-ass naked over there?" Virgie asked him. "Well, that's my daughter. If you don't get her out of here, I'm going to be back every night checking your bar license, and you know what that means."

Within minutes, the manager had Vickie dressed and Virgie put her daughter in the back of the patrol car and drove her away like a convict. They did not speak for the entire ride home. When they got back to the house, Vickie told her mom that she was making a thousand dollars a day stripping and that she needed the money for her son. She told her mother she'd never make that kind of money at the Red Lobster.

"My child ain't going to strip," Virgie said, putting her foot down.

Anna packed her bags and moved out and moved on to other strip joints, where managers didn't know about Virgie's law enforcement uniform. Vickie later took a job at Gigi's Cabaret, but she was considered too plump for the prime evening shifts, so she was relegated to the afternoon.

But it was while performing there—stripping against her mother's wishes—that Vickie Lynn Marshall was put on her path to stardom.

In 1991, during one fateful afternoon shift, "Miss Nikki," as she called herself, went over and talked to an elderly customer, billionaire oil tycoon J. Howard Marshall II, who was grieving the recent loss of both his wife and mistress. "I saw a very sick man," Anna has said, "and I just wanted to talk to him." He took an instant fancy to the 23-year-old and extended a lunch invitation for the following day. It would be her last shift at the strip club. The rest is tabloid history.

The following afternoon, at the end of their lunch, when beautiful "Nikki" announced that she had to get over to the club, Marshall passed across the table an envelope filled with money. And Miss Nikki, the stripper, was no more. "I was back with him the following day," she has recounted in interviews.

Things took off quickly. Within the week, the 86-year-old had proposed marriage. "I turned him down," she told Larry King. "I said that I had wanted to try and make something out of my life before [getting married]." The unlikely pair developed a caring, simpatico relationship (she thought he was sweet, he thought she was sexy) and he began supporting Vickie and her son Daniel.

Later that year, a determined Vickie Lynn Smith sent in nude photos of herself to *Playboy* magazine, expressing her interest in becoming a Playmate. According to *Playboy*, the editors were impressed enough to fly her out to Los Angeles for a test photo shoot. The results were mixed. *Playboy* Senior Contributing Photographer Arny Freytag "rejected her Playmate test," believing that "she had a great face, but she was overweight." Marilyn Grabowski, *Playboy* West Coast Photo Editor disagreed, saying, "You couldn't help but be mesmerized."

Vickie was chosen to be a Playmate, and made her debut on the March 1992 cover. Clad in a dark blue, strapless evening gown with a slit up the front, Vickie quickly captivated attention. Two months later, she became *Playboy*'s Miss May and had her first centerfold spread. For her first nude photo shoot, Anna was incredibly nervous. "I couldn't breathe," Anna exclaimed in an interview with *Entertainment Tonight*. "I couldn't eat breakfast. I was nauseated—I didn't know what was going to happen. I didn't know if I could go through with it." But she did, and her undeniable charisma shined through. On her centerfold mini-biography, she stated that she "wanted to become the next Marilyn Monroe."

In an unusual turn of events, *Playboy* denied Vickie a publicity tour. "We didn't do a publicity tour when she was Miss May, frankly because she sounded silly. She talked like a baby," Elizabeth Norris, former *Playboy* Director of Public Relations said. However, despite the lack of extra publicity, Vickie Smith quickly became one of the most talked about Playboy Playmates, and this voluptuous, full-figured woman got noticed big time.

Paul Marciano, president of Guess Jeans, approached Vickie shortly after her appearance in the March 1992 issue of *Playboy*. "I didn't know what Guess jeans were," Vickie said. This didn't stop her from signing on to be the new face of Guess, taking over from model Claudia Schiffer. "She brings back visions of Hollywood glamour," Guess photographer Daniela Federici told *People* magazine. "We haven't seen that kind of charisma since Marilyn Monroe."

It was while working with Marciano that Vickie decided—

like Norma Jeane Mortenson before her, who was successfully reborn as Marilyn Monroe—she needed to change her name. According to Anna, "Paul Marciano and me and one of his friends were sitting around coming up with a stage name, and that's where [the name] came from." With the new name, Anna Nicole's image of a rags-to-riches model and Playmate had become complete.

Meanwhile, Marshall showered Anna with gifts. Over the course of their courtship, Marshall gave Anna a fifteen-acre ranch, a car, endless amounts of cash, and on one specific shopping trip, two million dollars in Harry Winston jewelry. "He supported me 100 percent," Anna said.

According to her half brother, Donnie, the gifts didn't stop after Anna became famous. J. Howard Marshall loved shrimp and they'd always eat at Anna's old place of employment, the Red Lobster. In 1993, Donnie and Anna's newly reconnected dad, Donald Hogan, met Anna and J. Howard Marshall at the Red Lobster in Houston. After lunch, Mr. Marshall put on the table a box about the size of a candy box, and told her, "This is a gift." She opened the box in front of everyone. It was filled with $50,000 in crisp hundred-dollar bills wrapped in gold labels.

"You could tell he gave her the money because he wanted to," Donnie said. "She kissed him on the forehead. Then handed the dollars to her bodyguard." Donnie said before the lunch meeting, his sister pulled him aside, telling him that she didn't want J. Howard Marshall or his team to know she was dating anyone else. Donnie said she was very clear beforehand that "that's my bodyguard, not my boyfriend, remember?"

Her father told Donnie afterward, "Did you see that money? I wanted to grab it and run!"

"He [Marshall] was throwing money at my sister like it

was chump change," Donnie told me. "He had been ready to give up on life. She showed him that life is worth living. He went out with a bang marrying my sister."

After over two years of dating and gifts, Marshall again proposed to Anna, offering her a 22-carat engagement ring. She accepted. "I promised him that I would marry him after I made something of myself, and I got to where I was a name. And I promised him, and it was time to do something. And I wanted to have children." Remember, there was a sixty-plus year age difference between the two of them.

By this time, Anna was getting seen. She had a new name, a sexy image, and a highly coveted modeling contract. It seemed like her luck would never end. That year, Anna was named *Playboy*'s Playmate of the Year. On the cover, Anna wore little more than a piece of fabric to cover her breasts and in her interview she said, "I want to be the new Marilyn Monroe and find my own Clark Gable." At her Playmate of the Year party, she said, "It is a very big honor for me. I have always wanted this. I am just so happy and thrilled and I am so glad Mr. Hefner chose me."

"Her Playmate of the Year tour was first class all the way," Elizabeth Norris recalled. "She loved riding in limos and seeing all the cameras waiting for her." Hugh Hefner, the founder of *Playboy*, seemed to be quite proud of Anna. "There's something magic I think that happens between her and a camera," Hefner said in an *Entertainment Tonight* interview. "A lot of women are beautiful, but that kind of magic is special, and she has that."

But perhaps Anna got too caught up in her *Playboy* experiences, not knowing when to turn it on and turn it off. Donnie and her father met her once in a hotel room she was sharing with her bodyguard. She started stripping during lunch with her dad and brother present. According to Donnie, she took off her top and was about to take off her panties, when someone asked her what she was doing. "Oh sorry," she said. "I thought I was still at work. I work twelve hours a day."

In the midst of celebrating her successes, Anna kept her promise and married Marshall on June 27, 1994, at the White Dove Wedding Chapel in Houston. Because of his age and health, Marshall sat in his wheelchair, dressed in his all white tuxedo, waiting at the end of the aisle for Anna to come down. The wedding was very small; hardly anyone was there. Wearing a "long, hand-beaded wedding gown, with train and, of course, a plunging neckline," Anna walked on white rose-petals down the aisle. At the end of the ceremony, Anna and Marshall headed back up the aisle together. They then released two doves outside the chapel. Afterward, they fed each other cake and did a special champagne toast. The celebration, however, was short-lived. Friends and family members say Anna kissed her new husband goodbye and left for Greece with her bodyguard boyfriend, a bodyguard that her husband was reportedly paying for.

After the wedding, Anna had her modeling life in Los Angeles, and Marshall had his life in Texas where he continued to live. According to a security guard at a New Year's party at the Playboy Mansion, Anna was seen having sex in the pool and called the next day to say she lost her wedding ring. The security guard told me he found it and it was stored for six months before she picked it up.

But her friends and co-workers say despite Anna's antics, she always found time for Marshall. According to a *Playboy* interview with makeup artist Alexis Vogel, "Every day at 5 p.m. she would go into the models' lounge, a room off the studio with a couch and phone, to call him. They would talk for only a few minutes, but you could tell she was sweet on him."

"He called me his sleeping pill," Anna later told CNN. "Every night I had to call him."

According to an interview Anna's aunt, Elaine Tabor, did with ABC, "Anna Nicole [spent] days helping an 88-year-old man become a boy again, riding an all-terrain vehicle, living it up as if he had never aged." It seemed as if the twosome were showing each other a good time.

But the media wasn't quite as convinced of Anna's intentions in marrying Marshall. Tabloids frequently claimed that she had only married him for his money. "They think I'm a gold digger," Anna said. "And it's not true." Marshall's own son, Pierce Marshall, who at the time was almost twice as old as his step-mom Anna Nicole, was also not convinced at all. Pierce's lawyer, Rusty Hardin, says Anna was "unfaithful" to Marshall and that "she wanted to get as much from him as she could." He said, "I believe it's clear J. Howard loved her and she didn't love him."

Despite all the bad press and no matter what anyone else said, Anna firmly held that she truly loved Marshall. "I loved him for so much of what he did for me and my son," she told CNN. "I mean, I just loved him so—I've never had love like that before. No one has ever loved me and done things for me and respected me and didn't care about what people said about me. I mean, he truly loved me and I loved him for it." Anna claimed that she and Marshall even tried to have children. "We tried, but it didn't happen." The age difference might have been a logistical problem.

The whirlwind and controversy surrounding their relationship ended as quickly as it had begun. After only fourteen months of marriage, Marshall died of pneumonia on August 4, 1995. At his funeral, Anna wore her wedding dress.

The death of Marshall created Anna's biggest public fight:

was she or was she not entitled to inherit part of Marshall's massive estate? Was she a prostitute for pay or a rightfully married spouse? In his last will, Marshall declared that his son, Pierce, was to inherit his estate. However, Anna claimed that Marshall intended "to provide for her after his death, and set up a separate trust fund in her name." She began her battle for what she called her rightful claim to half of her late husband's $1.6 billion estate, money he amassed over the years from the oil and natural gas industry.

Rusty Hardin, the Marshall family attorney, says there is no evidence supporting these claims. However, in the midst of this legal battle, a video, made at Christmas shortly before Marshall's death, shows Vickie trying to get him to say something on the tape. "Say it just like you did last night," she said.

Marshall is then seen on-camera saying, "Vicky Nicole Smith shall receive the house, which she calls the ranch, and the townhouse, and her Mercedes automobile . . . and everything else that I have ever given her now and forever. I love you." This video became the subject of large debate concerning whether or not it entitled Anna to anything other than what she had already received. When Marshall initially died, the Texas probate court ruled that Anna Nicole should not get a cent of Marshall's fortune.

"There's no reference in that video to her getting half after his death, just that she keeps what he gave her when he was alive," Rusty Hardin explained. "This was never played before in court. If we get a new trial, we will bring that video in front row and center."

The case was left at the Texas court decision until 1996, when Anna filed for bankruptcy in the state of California after Maria Antonia Cerrato, her former housekeeper and babysitter, sued Anna for sexual harassment and was awarded a judgment of

$850,000. Since any money potentially due her from the Marshall estate would be considered part of her potential assets, the bankruptcy court got involved.

The case eventually went back and forth, up and down, between the Texas probate court and the California bankruptcy court until it forced the matter into federal court. According to the *Washington Post*, in 2002 "a bankruptcy court determined that she was entitled to $475 million, an award later reduced by U.S. District Judge David O. Carter to $88.5 million in damages from Pierce Marshall." The victory, however, was short lived. In December 2004, "a three-judge panel of the U.S. Court of Appeals for the 9th Circuit, based in San Francisco, threw out Judge Carter's ruling, declaring that only Texas's courts have jurisdiction."

In 2005, the U.S. Supreme Court decided to hear the appeal of that decision. The Bush administration even got involved, directing the Solicitor General to intercede on Smith's behalf out of an interest to expand federal court jurisdiction over state probate disputes. Finally, on May 1, 2006, a pregnant Anna Nicole Smith learned that the highest court in the land unanimously decided in Smith's favor. Justice Ruth Bader Ginsburg wrote the majority opinion and, though the decision did not give Smith any money, it affirmed her right to pursue her share of it in federal court.

On June 20, 2006, Anna's sixty-seven-year-old stepson, E. Pierce Marshall, died from an "aggressive infection." Attorney Rusty Hardin told me, "He was okay on Friday, celebrating the upcoming Father's Day with his family, then on Tuesday morning he was in a coma, and died that Tuesday afternoon."

His widow, Elaine T. Marshall, now represents the Marshall estate and says that she will continue to fight to prevent Anna's heirs from getting a dime. Rusty Hardin calls Howard K. Stern "a lawyer wannabe" and Hardin puts his own legal plans bluntly: "We'll fight this to the bitter end."

Regarding Larry Birkhead and Dannielynn ever seeing any of the Marshall fortune, Rusty Hardin says, "Give me a break." He explains it this way: "This is a case of a younger woman who marries a much older guy. She then sleeps with many different guys. One gets her pregnant. She moves out of the country to avoid him. She has the baby. Then she says to the family of the guy who used to be married to her, that it all goes to that new baby. This doesn't make any sense. This is outrageous. This baby is the product of a bunch of relationships and has nothing to do with J. Howard Marshall."

Throughout the ten years of fighting for the money, Anna became increasingly close to lawyer Howard K. Stern, a UCLA-trained lawyer who passed the bar in 1994. Anna and Stern, "met in 1996," according to Howard's testimony in that Florida courtroom with Judge Seidlin. It's been said that his good friend, Ron Rale, brought the two of them together. According to Rusty Hardin, "Anna has always been with attorneys who wanted big percentages of this deal."

In 2002, Howard told *Access Hollywood* "I kind of wear two different hats for Anna Nicole. One is lawyer and the other is friend." According to Jackie Hatten and other friends, Howard also played another role in Anna's life—gatekeeper, determining who would get access to her and who wouldn't. When she became pregnant, Howard was even more controlling about who was allowed to see her, even, and perhaps especially, the baby's father. Larry Birkhead told me that while Anna was pregnant, he had to "rescue her" at a hotel because Howard was giving her so much grief about Larry.

It was Howard who, when Anna was fighting for her late

husband's fortune, presented Anna's direct examination at trial. But Rusty Hardin said the real attorney leading the case to get Marshall's fortune is Philip Boesch with the Boesch Law Firm out of California. Rusty Hardin told me Boesch has been "my main nemesis on the Marshall case."

Howard K. Stern eventually dissolved his law firm. According to the *Seattle Times*, "By 2002, [Anna] was his only client. He never charged her for working as her personal lawyer . . . but Smith paid rent on his Santa Monica apartment and for everything they did together, sometimes giving him cash. [Former law partner Dave] Shebby says he and Stern had to end their brief partnership because Stern wasn't bringing in any income."

Soon after, Anna Nicole Smith created a company called Hot Smoochie Lips, Inc., which was run by Howard K. Stern. The company was shut down after the California Franchise Tax Board determined it owed more than $30,000 in back taxes. Howard also made numerous on-camera appearances on E!'s *The Anna Nicole Show* and did several television and interview appearances with her.

For the record, according to his own court testimony, the most Howard has made as Anna's attorney since 2002 was during his participation in Anna's reality show. He was paid $12,500 or less a year for his involvement on the show. By 2006, he has said, he had no job, "I was with Anna." He never charged her for legal expenses, but she paid for his apartment in Santa Monica, his clothes, his shoes, and gave him money, and, according to Stern, even let him sign her checks. During the court testimony in Florida, thirty-eight-year-old Howard also said that his parents have been giving him money.

It was while Anna was entrenched in the legal battles that she decided she needed to start making money again, so she started hitting the pavement once more. Anna told *Entertainment Weekly*: "I finally got to a point where I could work again. I was like, hmmm, I love cameras. So, why not? Let's go for it." With this, *The Anna Nicole Show* was created, and in 2002, Anna's reality television debut premiered on the E! Entertainment Television. According to *Entertainment Weekly*, "the show's August debut scored 7.6 million viewers, marking E!'s best numbers ever and the best debut for a reality show in cable history."

Executive vice president of E!, Mark Sonnenberg, said in a 2002 *Entertainment Weekly* story that "there's a circus atmosphere that will attract people [to *The Anna Nicole Show*]. Here's a single mother who's been struggling to make it while taking on the rich and powerful to make a better life for her and her son. She's also a grieving widow. When you watch and spend time with her, she's very captivating."

The Anna Nicole Show was promoted as "it's not supposed to be funny, it just is." During its two-season run, *The Anna Nicole Show* chronicled the infamous model's life, detailing such activities as trips to the dentist and driving lessons. Everything, from eating contests to bringing home the ashes of her late husband J. Howard Marshall, was captured on camera.

Along with Anna, Howard K. Stern "served as a kind of valet," according to the *Seattle Times*. "Stern is continually fetching things. Smith sits while he brings her food from the buffet, and then she complains he didn't bring everything she wanted. He carries her bags and smiles when, at one point, she shoves him. His shirt is always untucked, his eyes too eager. He often totes her small dog, Sugar Pie."

Also included on the show were Anna's son Daniel (who didn't seem to appreciate the cameras around), her interior designer Bobby Trendy, and her assistant Kim (who got a tattoo of Anna on her arm).

One of the most interesting aspects of the show is Anna's struggle with her weight. According to *TIME* magazine, "Smith's weight increased during her inheritance case; she became addicted to painkillers and had a bout of depression." During the show's run, "Smith's five-bedroom, 4,700-sq.-ft. rented house in the San Fernando Valley is stocked with a Costco's worth of Kraft Easy Mac, pizza-flavored Pringles, Handi-Snacks and Cheetos."

Anna's weight became a problem. She couldn't lose the pounds that E! wanted her to and, after two seasons, her show wasn't renewed. In 2003, she signed on to become a spokesperson for TrimSpa and by the following year had lost a reported eighty pounds, transforming her body back to her early nineties perfection.

In November 2004, she revealed her new body during a now legendary appearance at the American Music Awards. During her introduction of the next musical performance on the live show, Anna's speech was visibly slurred and her behavior was bizarre. She threw her arms up and exclaimed, "Like my body?"

Now knowing Anna Nicole's medical history, experts like Dr. Keith Eddleman at New York's Mount Sinai Hospital say that her "slurred speech and exaggerated behaviors may have been indicative of someone taking methadone. It has the same euphoric effects as heroin."

The following day her appearance at the American Music Awards was played over and over again around the world. Though *The Anna Nicole Show* was no longer on-air, her exploits and foibles continued off-camera. Her life, like her show, wasn't meant to be funny. And now, on February 8, 2007, it really wasn't. Anna Nicole Smith was dead.

CHAPTER 9

The Body

IN MY ALMOST TWENTY YEARS OF JOURNALISM, COVERING STO-
ries from the Michael Jackson molestation trial to President
Clinton's impeachment, I have never seen anything like the
media swarm that circled the body of Anna Nicole Smith. The
day after she died, satellite trucks, helicopters, squad cars, a
mob scene the likes of which had never been seen before, hit
Fort Lauderdale. The normally quiet medical examiner's office
where forensic pathologist Dr. Joshua Perper, Chief Medical
Examiner of Broward County toiled, was now squarely in the
media crosshairs. Like the pounding rain that slams Floridians
each year, this storm grew into a full-fledged Hurricane Anna.

Lying on a gurney in the building that served as a backdrop
for the news conference, Anna Nicole's voluptuous body had
just been dissected by Dr. Joshua Perper. He speaks with a Romanian accent, and is an endearing combination of wacky
scientist and gentle grandfather. The crowd fell suddenly quiet
as he stepped to the microphone to make his initial statements

before the press about this case. Right away, reporters zeroed in on prescription drugs and who may have given them to her. As you'll see from his answers—only twenty-four hours after she was pronounced dead—details of what happened inside room 607 and inside the body of Anna Nicole Smith were conflicting and hard to ascertain.

February 9, 3:10 p.m.

DR. JOSHUA PERPER, BROWARD COUNTY, FLORIDA, CHIEF MEDICAL EXAMINER: Good afternoon. . . . I would like, first, to thank Chief Tiger from the Seminole police, who did a very professional investigation in this particular case. . . . We will have the— Chief Charlie Tiger say a few words about his investigation. And, then, I will report to you about our findings.

CHARLIE TIGER, SEMINOLE, FLORIDA, POLICE CHIEF: . . . First, I want to again extend our sympathy to the family and friends of Anna Nicole Smith. . . .

With regard to the ongoing investigation, we have some additional information we—to share with you today. At the Seminole Police Department, we treat any death with utmost importance, and investigate it thoroughly. At this point, no evidence has been revealed to suggest that a crime occurred. We found no illegal drugs, only prescription medicines. We are not releasing the names on those prescriptions.

We have taken sworn statements from all the parties involved. Everyone has cooperated fully. We are continuing to review certain surveillance tapes, but nothing unusual has been observed. This incident will remain open, an open investigation, until all tests are completed by the medical examiner's office. Thank you for being here today.

DR. JOSHUA PERPER: We have been informed that yesterday was—February 8th at about 1:00 p.m. or around it, the attendants of Mrs. Nicole Smith found her collapsed and unconscious. She apparently had been sick for several days with what was approximately some kind of stomach flu. And one of the individuals who was a bodyguard, provided resuscitation. Medics came to the scene and the body was transferred to the hospital. In the hospital, unfortunately, the patient was virtually dead on arrival and was declared dead around 2:40 or so in the afternoon.

According to the Florida statute, the Broward County Medical Examiner assumed jurisdiction because this is clearly a sudden, unexpected and unexplained death. And according to that, myself and one of our associate medical examiners, Dr. Juste, performed an autopsy, which we just completed several moments ago.

The autopsy was able to exclude any kind of physical injury, such as blunt force trauma, gunshot wound, stab wounds or asphyxia as a cause of death, as a contributory cause of death or a hastening cause of death.

The only thing which we found in terms of very minor trauma was a minor bruise on the back, which was related apparently to a fall reported to have occurred several days ago while the—Mrs. Smith was in the bathroom. The autopsy revealed only subtle findings in the heart and in the gastrointestinal system, in other words, in the intestines, which would have to be verified microscopically. The other finding, which we found was a small amount of blood in the stomach, which is related to her being in terminal shock a short time before she died.

At this time, we do not make a determination of the cause and the manner of death. And, basically, we have a long list of investigation procedures which have to be completed and include an extensive review of the medical records, interview the witnesses which were with Mrs. Smith or witnessed her collapse, further cardiovascular examination of the heart and neuropathological examination of the brain and the spinal cord, bacterial and viral studies of the heart, intestines and a variety of other tissues, chemical analysis of the eye fluid and an extensive microscopic examination of the body tissues which were taken for examination.

Now, it's our estimate that collecting the information and putting it together and relating the clinical, pathological and laboratory data would take approximately somewhere between three and five weeks.

The medical examiner's office is obviously aware of the significant public interest in this death and therefore, we are prepared to make optimal efforts to expedite the determination of the cause and manner of death without affecting the thoroughness and the reliability of our investigation.

So, now, if you have any questions, either address the chief or to me.

(REPORTERS BEGAN TO RIDDLE HIM WITH QUESTIONS. OUR JOB IS TO RAISE ANY RED FLAGS. OFTEN TIMES, AT PRESS CONFERENCES SUCH AS THIS, THE LOUDEST, MOST DOGGED REPORTER IS THE ONE WHO GETS HIS OR HER QUESTION HEARD, IF NOT ANSWERED.)

QUESTION: Is there any indication that she may have taken a large amount of the prescription drugs that were in the room? And what were those drugs, please?

PERPER: There is no such indication because we didn't find any kind of pills in the stomach. If this would be the case, then there would have been a large amount. We would have seen that. However, at this time, we don't have the results of the chemical tests, of the toxicological tests. And that's why this determination of the cause and manner of death is postponed until the entire—pieces of the puzzle. It's a medical puzzle which you have to resolve, have to be placed in place so we get a comprehensive picture of what exactly happened.

QUESTION: Have you ruled out drugs?

PERPER: No, I didn't rule it. I think I was very clear. What I said is that as part of our investigation, we will make a very comprehensive and thorough examination of a variety of drugs and medication, which she probably took. We have a list of the medication, which apparently were in the room. But the list of medication doesn't mean that those medications would be found in the person. So we did not exclude any kind of contribution of medication for the death. And this will have to wait for the results of the toxicological study.

QUESTION: Are you ruling out that it was a natural cause of death?

PERPER: It's a possibility that it might be. At this time, I cannot make a determination because there are a number of possibilities. Basically, there are three major possibilities. One is that the death is due solely to natural causes. The other possibility is that the death might be due to some medication or chemicals. And the third possibility is that there's a combination of natural causes and medication and at this time, we do not have the results of the test, which would permit us to make this determination.

QUESTION: Doctor Perper, you said there was a subtle finding—you found subtle findings in the heart and gastrointestinal that need additional further examination. But what could those findings be an indication of?

PERPER: Well, sometimes findings—very subtle findings in the heart can be an indication of an inflammatory process in the heart, which is not visible by the naked eye. That's why I'm saying—I'm not saying that I made this diagnosis. But I see something, which looks a little bit unusual and on microscopic examination this may verify a significant process or it may be nothing.

QUESTION: You were talking about those injuries. Did they come from continued drug abuse?

PERPER: I don't—no, there are no findings to indicate continuous drug abuse.

QUESTION: OK. We were hearing she may have passed away because of vomiting. Did she choke on her own vomit? That's the theory we're hearing out there.

PERPER: Well, we found in the stomach a small amount of blood, as I said before. This small amount of blood we related to a terminal event of shock. And the reason is that from the stomach, the contents of what an individual is ingesting go in the intestine. And we did not find blood in the intestine, but we found some intestinal contents. So it means that what is the blood occurred very shortly before the death.

We didn't find in the stomach any kind of tablets or pills. And we did not find evidence by the naked eye, by the gross examination that was chronic abuse. However, at this time, as I said, our findings are limited to what we are able to see with our eyes . . . .

QUESTION: Chief Tiger, what about the rumors that when paramedics arrived in the room, they witnessed Mr. Stern flushing the toilet?

TIGER: None of our officers that arrived on the scene saw anything like that at all.

QUESTION: How about the paramedics?

TIGER: They didn't see anything like that also.

QUESTION: Chief, are you guys going to be releasing that 911 call?

TIGER: The call that came into our office, we're not going to release at this time.

QUESTION: Doctor, is it possible for someone to have died from an overdose if you do not find any pills in her stomach?

PERPER: It's possible. As I said at this point, we do not—I don't have any information one way or another which I can reliably relate to you. That's what I explained. Usually, we don't do this kind of press conference, but because I wanted to prevent rumor from spreading and particularly rumors which are incorrect. I wanted to make you know what our findings are and that additional findings will come as the tests will come in.

QUESTION: Doctor, based on the body temperature at the hospital, could she have been dead for hours before?

PERPER: No. And the reason is that according to our information at the time when the medics came to the scene, the body was warm and there were no indications that a long time occurred since the body was found.

147

QUESTION: Do you know what the funeral plans are? Where the body is going?

PERPER: Not yet. But that's information which is . . .

QUESTION: How long did the autopsy take?

PERPER: Well it's hard to say because if we start from the very test, which was started until we ended, we started about 9:30 and we just finished, so approximately six hours.

QUESTION: And also will the body be held here for the 10 days until the court hearing?

PERPER: We always comply with court orders and we try to be cooperative with the family. If we are going to be asked, we will do that for them.

QUESTION: You mentioned that she had been sick for several days with the stomach flu. Was there anything else unusual that had happened in those days leading up to this? And also did she spend the day in bed or was she up and about?

PERPER: My understand—one of the things which I mentioned that I'm going to do and I did not do yet is not just review the medical records but to speak with the witnesses who took care of her. So this is a legitimate question, which I'm going to ask.

QUESTION: You mentioned no pills in the stomach, but could she have had some sort of liquid and/or inhaled something that could have caused it?

Anna had always dreamed of having a baby girl. When she finally did,
figuring out who would be named as the father took a lot of
behind-the-scenes negotiation.
[GETTY IMAGES]

One month before he died, Anna's son, Daniel, met a private investigator at Paty's restaurant in Los Angeles County and told him he was "deathly afraid" of Howard K. Stern. [AUTHOR COLLECTION]

Hours after arriving in the Bahamas to meet his new baby sister, Daniel died mysteriously in his mom's hospital bed. [GETTY IMAGES]

Daniel's godmother, Jackie Hatten, rushed down to the Bahamas, worried that Anna could be next. [NYGARD INTERNATIONAL]

The Horizons House, where Anna and Howard were living, had become a fortress. Jackie Hatten didn't get past the intercom box to the left of the gate. [AUTHOR COLLECTION]

Anna's Bahamian attorney thought her commitment ceremony with Howard was nothing more than a publicity stunt. In attendance was Moe Brighthaupt, Anna's bodyguard, who months later gave Anna her last rites.
[Getty Images]

Anna really married J. Howard Marshall II, who was six decades her senior. Her child, little Dannielynn, could now inherit half of his billion-dollar fortune.
[© Corbis]

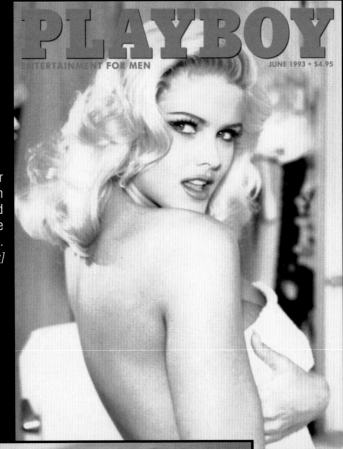

PLAYBOY

ENTERTAINMENT FOR MEN

JUNE 1993 • $4.95

Anna's career skyrocketed when she was named Playmate of the Year in 1993.
[© CORBIS]

Anna was often seen at the top Hollywood events, including Peter Nygard's Oscars gala. She dated the fashion mogul for three years and became one of his top models.
[NYGARD INTERNATIONAL]

Anna often spent time together with Larry Birkhead and Howard,
including dressing up at Hugh Hefner's Halloween party at the
Playboy Mansion in 2004.
[© CORBIS]

Howard always
had his camera ready
to get the shot.
The last time Anna
Nicole would be seen
at a public event
was at a January 2007
boxing match at the
Hard Rock Hotel.
[© CORBIS]

Anna was found unconscious and not breathing in a four-poster, king-size bed in room 607 at the Hard Rock Hotel in Hollywood, Florida.
[AP IMAGES/LYNNE SLADKY]

Brigitte Neven and King Eric Gibson were there at the critical moments: She was the first to discover Anna's lifeless body. He was with Howard when he got the fateful call.
[AUTHOR COLLECTION]

Oddly, the morning of Anna's death, workers at her new Bahamian house failed to show up to finish spraying the darker pink stucco on the exterior. They have not returned since.
[AUTHOR COLLECTION]

An emotional Virgie Arthur, Anna's mother, said she won't rest until she feels Dannielynn is safe, adding, "God help them when they have to stand before God."
[*AUTHOR COLLECTION*]

Even though Howard K. Stern testified on the stand that he was the father of Dannielynn, he privately made this offer to Larry: "I will give you your baby if you leave me as executor of the estate."
[*© CORBIS*]

The moment of unity between the parties was short-lived, as, hours later, Larry and Howard met secretly at a Florida hotel. Virgie and others think Larry made a deal.
[*© CORBIS*]

During Larry's time in Florida and the Bahamas, the author had a unique perspective of events, often sharing dinner with him after the day's proceedings.
[*AUTHOR COLLECTION*]

On March 26, 2007, Medical Examiner Dr. Joshua Perper and Seminole Police Chief Charlie Tiger announced that Anna Nicole Smith had died of "an accidental overdose" and "found nothing to indicate any foul play." [AUTHOR COLLECTION]

Outside the medical examiner's office, a small shrine was set up to remember the starlet's life. [AUTHOR COLLECTION]

The hearse carrying Anna is escorted by her bodyguards. [AUTHOR COLLECTION]

Some of Anna's friends thought a small private church funeral was the last thing Anna would have picked for herself. "She would have wanted people walking by the casket for days," Peter Nygard said. [AUTHOR COLLECTION] INSET: Larry Birkhead is seen leaving Anna's funeral. To his left is Mark Speer, from his security detail, who was present for many of Larry's revealing conversations. [AUTHOR COLLECTION]

PERPER: Well, we are going to check those possibilities because we are going to test the stomach content and as with an inhalant, we are going to test the lungs for any inhalants.

QUESTION: There was prescribed medication?

PERPER: Right.

QUESTION: Was it in her name or someone else's name?

PERPER: I did not see it myself. I cannot answer the question.

UNIDENTIFIED MALE: Chief Tiger, do you want to know whether or not she was prescribed the medications that were in her room?

TIGER: We'll find that out through our investigation. It's still ongoing.

QUESTION: Chief, what was in those bags you removed yesterday? Those bags you took out yesterday? What was in those bags?

TIGER: Evidence from the scene.

QUESTION: Why did she have a private nurse?

TIGER: We're not ready to discuss that right now.

QUESTION: Chief, why did she have a private nurse with her?

PERPER: As I explained to you, there is additional information which has to be elicited from the people

149

who took care of her. There was a nurse apparently also in the room or close to her. I'm going to question this nurse as to what happened.

QUESTION: Hasn't he questioned the nurse? Hasn't he already or the police department? The question is, why did she have a private nurse?

PERPER: But I'm going to question. There are two types of questioning. There is medical questioning and non-medical questioning. The police did its own non-medical questioning. I'll do the medical one and I'm going to ask all of the proper questions and this is the . . .

QUESTION: Would you characterize the amount of drugs that were found in her room as excessive for one person?

PERPER: I didn't make this determination. I don't know, I didn't look at the fact—and the fact is that people sometimes have medication, which they have for a long time and they don't take them.

QUESTION: Large amount?

PERPER: This is something which, again, has to be determined, yes. The problem is not how many medications are in the bottles. The problem or the significant thing is how many medications are in her body. Whatever is in the bottle, it's irrelevant. But what is in her body is very significant.

QUESTION: From what you've seen of the types of those pills in combination, could it have been lethal?

PERPER: I—if you—have a combination of any drugs in the body, if you have five bottles of drugs, you are going to take everything in the bottle, you'll get in trouble. It's not a legitimate question.

QUESTION: Doctor Perper, do you know why a doctor visited Anna earlier this week?

PERPER: I do not know because I did not review yet the medical records. Part of the investigation, part of the information which has to be obtained in order to solve the puzzle is exactly her medical condition, the kind of procedure which she had, the kind of medication that she took, how much she was prescribed . . . .

QUESTION: But you will be reviewing the medical records?

PERPER: Absolutely.

QUESTION: How many different medications were found in the body?

PERPER: I cannot give you a list now. Something to review. There were a number of them.

QUESTION: Doctor, one more question please.

OFFICIAL: Thank you very much. Thank you very much. Thank you.

QUESTION: Where is Howard Stern?

Though he was accommodating to the reporters' inquiries, Dr. Perper acknowledged that there were a lot of unanswered questions. The toxicology report would take weeks, and reporters were made even more anxious by the inconclusive assessments thus far. Reporters immediately drew comparisons to the privately commissioned autopsy on the body of Anna's son Daniel—less than 120 days prior in the Bahamas—which revealed a lethal combination of methadone and two anti-depressants.

Reporters wondered right away if Anna's death was more than an eerie parallel. In fact, Anna had been taking a medley of prescription medication for years and had severe and highly publicized drug combination problems before. One 1995 incident put her in a wheelchair on the grounds of the Betty Ford Clinic, leaving her spokesperson to explain that "Ms. Smith is convalescing in a private location" after a previous hospitalization that was described as resulting from "an adverse reaction to two prescription medications."

But numerous friends and boyfriends over the years have expressed their concerns. Though Peter Nygard said he never actually saw Anna take drugs, he started seeing packages being sent to her in the mail with prescriptions in them. He questioned her and wouldn't give her the packages. "She would get pissed off at me when she found out I wasn't passing along her prescriptions," Peter told me. "And we'd always fight about it."

"You can't do this," she'd whine. "I need my drugs."

But sadly, by February 8, 2007, Anna's body had become a over-medicated depository of an unbelievably astonishing quantity of drugs.

According to Reuters, more than 1,800 pills and a bottle of the powerful sedative "chloral hydrate" had been prescribed by Anna's psychiatrist, Dr. Eroshevich, in the five weeks before Anna Nicole Smith met her untimely death. Of all the drugs Dr. Eroshevich prescribed, eight of them, including the chloral hydrate, had prescriptions written to Howard K. Stern, two of them were prescribed to Alex Katz, and one of the drugs found in the room, potassium chloride, was prescribed by Dr. Khris to herself. The Federal Drug Enforcement Agency and the Medical Board of California have been investigating Dr. Khris and Dr. Sandeep Kapoor for misconduct relating to Anna Nicole Smith's over-medication. Dr. Kapoor is the Los Angeles doctor who prescribed her methadone while she was pregnant.

Eventually, Dr. Perper said of all the medications found in Anna's system, none of the drugs found in her body were in lethal levels on their own. However, he said the "combination" of so many of them led to a toxic, and, ultimately, lethal effect. The chloral hydrate, the same sleeping medication that, ironically and coincidentally, contributed to the 1962 death of Anna's idol Marilyn Monroe, most likely "tipped the balance" and led to a combined medication overdose for Smith as well.

Chloral hydrate was one of the first sleeping medications out there. It acts as a depressant on the central nervous system. Popular in the 1930s, it was also called "knockout drops." If you put some in an alcoholic drink it became known as a "Mickey Finn."

Dr. Michael Baden, an internationally renowned forensic expert and former chief medical examiner of New York City, told Fox News that the normal dosage for chloral hydrate would be around 500 milligrams a day; yet Anna was taking more than 5,000 milligrams a day for the last 37 days of her life. Dr. Baden has also pointed out that the drug Soma (Carisoprodol), a muscle relaxant that Anna Nicole was taking, has a recommended daily dosage of four pills a day. Anna was taking twenty a day. You may remember that a Carisoprodol tablet was found in the hospital room bed where Howard K. Stern had slept the night Daniel arrived. Anna Nicole was also continuing to take methadone. The medical examiner's report says it wasn't found in her blood and urine, but it was found in her bile, which "is an indication that the methadone had not been administered for at least two to three days before death."

Since at the time of their deaths both Anna and her son had methadone in their system, Baden feels the Drug Enforcement Agency should be interested. "They [the DEA] are very strict on how that can be prescribed," Baden said. "And I think that whoever then took the drug, the chloral hydrate, and gave it to Anna Nicole that she died from, could also be in some trouble, civil and criminal."

The day of Dr. Perper's press conference, the Center for Disease Control released a report that said unintentional fatal drug overdoses are the second-leading cause of accidental death, just after car wrecks. The rate of fatal drug overdoses nearly doubled from 1999 to 2004, from 11,155 to 19,833. CDC researchers say they believe sedatives and prescription pain-killers were the chief cause of the increase.

In commenting about Anna's case specifically, Dr. Baden noted, "If any of the drugs in her system were illegally obtained, the person who gave them to her could be held responsible."

• • •

After Dr. Perper's news conference ended, I lingered to talk further with the man who had just examined Anna Nicole inside and out. He and I connected over our Slovakian background—he's Romanian and I'm Polish—and we talked about his time in Romania, of his family and his life. Then, I asked for a tour of the autopsy room where he had just completed the examination of Anna Nicole Smith's body. He took me into the huge, sterile room not far from his first-floor office. His colleagues had just finished the procedure on Anna Nicole and were, in fact, still cleaning up. I saw scalpels, saws, and stainless steel gurneys—reminiscent of the set on TV's *CSI*. They had just cut into the body of this beautiful 39-year-old woman.

Anna Nicole Smith's body—her vehicle to fame and misfortune—at death was, according to Dr. Perper, that of a "well-developed, well-nourished" woman. She was five feet, eleven inches in length and weighed 178 pounds.

According to his autopsy, "The scalp hair is blonde and measures up to five inches in length in the frontal area and up to 19 inches in length in the back and on top of her head. There are multiple blonde hair extensions including several pink strands attached to the natural hair, which shows light brown roots."

The world famous blonde actually had brown hair.

Anna Nicole's famous breasts were, as most of us realized, as unnatural as her blonde hair. She had breast implants, each containing 700ml of clear fluid. A $14,000 gift from her husband J. Howard Marshall, she had wanted them big. Really big. Long rumored to be the work of a famous Texas plastic surgeon, her 42DD breasts caused her a lot of back pain. Friends say this is the pain that started her taking prescription medications. Dr. Perper noted—as did several boyfriends I interviewed—that her left nipple was disfigured, almost to the point of mutilation, ironic for a woman whose naked body earned her the title of *Playboy*'s Playmate of the Year.

Anna's body, much like her persona, was quite colorful. She had numerous tattoos, including a pair of red lips on her abdomen, two cherries on her right hip, and a Playboy Bunny on her left. Laying across her lower back, Dr. Perper noted a mermaid on a flower bed with a pair of lips beneath it. Covering a cluster of small scars on her right leg and ankle was an icon medley—Christ's head, Our Lady of Guadalupe, the Holy Bible, the naked torso of a woman, the smiling face of Marilyn Monroe, a heart, shooting flames, and a cross. But perhaps the strangest tattoos—the words "Daniel" and "Papas," the names of her son and her octogenarian husband—were intricately and painfully placed above her pelvic bone. "The two people she cared about and truly loved," Jackie Hatten said.

She had piercings both above and below her belly button and her "buttocks have inconspicuous small scars, bilaterally." Anna Nicole, national spokesperson for TrimSpa, had liposuction. According to friend Jackie Hatten, she had five liposuction procedures. At least two of them occurred between the time when an overweight Anna Nicole Smith joined TrimSpa, to when she appeared on TV newly slender and sleek. Jackie says she accompanied her to a private outpatient clinic in Newport Beach, California, where Anna had liposuction. Following the procedure, Anna laid in bed for a month wrapped in a girdle and towels, to help her sagging skin recover from liposuction, and, Jackie says, Anna was drinking . . . Slimfast.

Besides what appears to be liposuction scars on Anna's buttocks, there was also "subcutaneous scarring" in several spots found during Anna's autopsy from "continuous injections." But the real cause for concern was a 3×2.5×2 centimeter puss-filled abscess on the left buttock from a needle injection. According to Dr. Perper, this sore was the cause of her raging 105 degree fever and the need for antibiotics. "The infectious organisms reached the bloodstream and caused an elevated temperature," Dr. Perper surmised. The needle puncturing into Anna Nicole's buttock allowed bacteria to get into her blood.

Dr. Perper theorized that Anna could have lived had she sought simple treatment for the fever and infection at a hospital. There she would have gotten immediate care and most likely would not have had the opportunity to take chloral hydrate, which tipped the balance. Anna's refusal to go to the hospital or have someone call 911 was indulged by her physician, by her lawyer-"husband," and by her bodyguard, all of whom were supposed to have her best interests at heart. Instead, they chose not to override the wishes of their obviously, extremely ill patient. Remember, only two months prior, King Eric was able to get her to go to the doctor when her back hurt, simply by asking her to go and telling her he and Howard would go with her.

So it seems Anna could be alive today if one of these three—psychiatrist Dr. Khris Eroshevich, lawyer Howard K. Stern, or bodyguard Moe Brighthaupt—had compelled her to do the same.

● ● ●

After my tour of the Broward County medical examination facility, I asked Dr. Perper where the body of Anna Nicole was now being kept. Dr. Perper told me he was worried about someone taking or damaging the body, so he had undertaken extreme measures to make sure Anna Nicole Smith was secure. She had been placed in a V.I.P. section within a series of vaults and under 24-hour guard.

"While the body is in my possession," he said, "she will be safe."

CHAPTER 10

The Fight for Anna

I FIRST MET ANNA NICOLE SMITH AT FASHION MAGNATE PETER Nygard's chic Los Angeles "The Night of 100 Stars" Oscars gala, annually held at the famous Beverly Hills Hotel. One of the premiere parties for Hollywood legends, both young and old, it's the event where he and Anna originally met and clicked right away. Peter had a romantic relationship with Anna that ended, he says, because of her addiction to drugs.

"She was sweet, she was afraid, a nice person," Peter said. "She didn't have a mean bone in her body and was crying out for help in my opinion. She tried to reach out for somebody who would help her."

"She did lead a fast life," said her former publicist David Granoff. "When she was good, she was very good. When she was bad, she was very bad."

The night I met Anna there were many well-known celebrities at Peter Nygard's party—but the moment Anna Nicole descended the long staircase, heads turned, conversations

158

stopped. She knew how to make a grand entrance and cameras were ready. Hers was a different presence, unmistakable and palpable. Her hair was up and she was wearing a slinky, form-fitting floral-printed dress showcasing her trademark cleavage. Her aura filled the room like a whirling tornado, an intense combination of raw sexual energy and uncanny social insecurity.

She recognized me and came over. "Hi, I'm Anna Nicole," she said. As I kissed her cheek, I remember thinking that hiding beneath all that hair and makeup was actually someone very sweet, authentic, and deeply afraid. She wanted to make sure everyone knew she was there, but it was more than that. She also wanted everyone to like her and to recognize her as an object of beauty.

After her death, as her body waited in a vault under heavy guard, Anna Nicole Smith had become just an object. An object that now, even in death, the world wanted to know who would lay claim to her and take her home.

Broward County Circus

The spotlight in the Anna Nicole Show now turned to the court fight over possession and burial of the star's body. During six days in February 2007, Judge Larry Seidlin, a family court judge with the Broward County Circuit, was the ringleader of an intensely emotional hearing for all sides. Virgie Arthur and Larry Birkhead were a team. Or so Virgie thought. They hugged before court and vowed to pull out everything in their personal arsenal to stop Howard Stern from controlling not just Anna's body, but also her estate. Larry was testifying as a witness for Virgie.

Each morning, the melee that awaited the participants when they arrived at the courthouse—and for Judge Larry Seidlin's jarring wisecracks—was a clamoring chaos. The media climbed on top of each other to get one or two words from one of the three parties—Howard K. Stern, Larry Birkhead, and Virgie Arthur—or as Judge Seidlin referred to them "Stern," "Larry," and "Mama." He called their respective legal teams "Florida," "California," and "Texas."

When I asked Larry Birkhead what he hoped for his day in court, he said, "I expect for the truth to come out and to respect Anna's wishes."

What Anna Nicole got was a riveting televised courtroom drama of mixed metaphors, strange analogies, and a judge who seemed to dramatize his delivery for the camera, playing every second of his fifteen-minutes of fame. Judge Seidlin proved to be as colorful as the other characters involved in the circus, though his feathers were ruffled at the mention of the word "circus."

Judge Seidlin often let the proceedings get off track by putting himself into the testimony. In one memorable, rather disjointed exchange with participants, he said: "There's no circus here, my friend. There's no circus here. This is life. We all come with some broken suitcases. Let's face it—money is the root of all evil. Am I right? When I used to teach tennis, I used to wear white shorts and a white top. It always looked good. You look good. Instead of fighting, you should join hands. Join hands, because it's only in this country that you can join hands. We don't have these kinds of religious wars and all these other issues that take place around the world." He'd proffer his wisdom, and then delve into far-fetched talk, such as his wardrobe, his young daughter, or his Bronx roots, where he was once a New York City cab driver.

The basic legal question, however, was where Anna Nicole Smith wanted to be buried and who should be considered the "next of kin." But as Dan Abrams, general manager of MSNBC asked, "Why are we going into drug use, and who had relationships with who? It doesn't make any sense."

Many observers felt that the judge made a mockery of the system, perhaps in pursuit of his own legal reality TV show. "Ninety or 95 percent of this hearing is totally irrelevant," Miami defense attorney Roy Black said on NBC's *Today Show*. "We are going into murder, money, drugs, and lots of sex. What does that have to do with the issue? The issue is: Where did she want to be buried?"

The Drugs

During the week, cameras captured plenty of tears from each of the concerned parties—Howard K. Stern, Larry Birkhead, and Virgie Arthur. There was a sense of vulnerability and overwhelming sadness from both Larry and Virgie, both of whom said emphatically that they wished Anna Nicole would have listened to their pleas to stop her drug use.

Howard K. Stern, according to many legal analysts, gave very ambiguous answers when it came to Anna's prescription drugs. When the judge asked him if Anna abused drugs, Howard said, "I'm not a doctor." When asked by the judge if he could have gotten Anna off drugs, it did not go unnoticed that Howard was vague.

According to Larry Birkhead's testimony, he had asked Anna Nicole to go to a drug rehabilitation facility in order to detoxify and overcome the addiction he felt she had to prescription drugs. Anna had told him, "I'm not a drug addict and quit calling me one." Or she would argue, "These are prescriptions." Larry said he responded, "You're not taking them properly." He told the court, "It was her contention because there was a doctor's name on the bottle, that there was nothing wrong with whatever she could take."

Larry Birkhead recounted that at one point during her pregnancy Anna Nicole Smith was in the hospital for around two weeks for detox to get her weaned off prescription drugs.

LARRY BIRKHEAD: At one point during the stay in the hospital she asked me to go get some personal belongings out of the closet in the hospital. And when I went into the closet, she asked me to bring the bag out. And she kept pushing the buttons for the drugs to come out, and she was getting frustrated and she kept telling me to press the nurse to tell her to get more, and I said, "You've had enough. They said you can't have anymore." And she goes, "I need more." And then when she told me to get her bag for something totally unrelated to drugs, like a toothbrush or something like that, she came back—when I brought the bag back to her, they— she pulled the bottle out.

[Ears perked up in the courtroom as Anna's boyfriend recounted the drug scene in the hospital. "They" was an interesting choice of words for Larry Birkhead. He also noticed he had said "they," and Larry felt the need to explain.]

LARRY BIRKHEAD: Mr. Stern was in the room, and they were waiting to see who came in, and they opened the bottle, and it was . . .

JUDGE SEIDLIN: "They" opened the bottle? Did Anna open the bottle, or did Mr. Stern open the bottle? "They" didn't open a bottle.

BIRKHEAD: Well, it happened multiple times. So I guess he did and she did both, and I witnessed both.

JUDGE SEIDLIN: And what did do you?

BIRKHEAD: I told them not to.

JUDGE SEIDLIN: Don't make it compound. What did you do next if anything?

BIRKHEAD: I told them not to, and repeatedly told her not to. And I watched and I stayed up for almost 24 hours a day to make sure that she didn't. And then when I made it another point to say something when she ripped her IV cord out of her arm, they told me to leave. And then later, I came out and found out she was on suicide watch. That's what I did.

JUDGE SEIDLIN: Then what did do you?

BIRKHEAD: I was asked to leave. She asked me to leave the hospital or she was going to call the nurse, because I was trying to make her stop.

JUDGE SEIDLIN: Why did you leave?

BIRKHEAD: Because she told me if I didn't, they were going to call security on me, the hospital. And I told

Howard what was going on. He says, it's best if you just go, she's not in her right mind. And they had a nurse sitting there 24 hours a day, the room was crowded up and they asked me to leave—they told me to leave.

JUDGE SEIDLIN: Do you think Howard provided—for Miss Anna Nicole Smith, do you think he provided some kind of support system for her?

BIRKHEAD: Support system in enabling? Or support . . .

JUDGE SEIDLIN: No, no, no. I'm not talking about enabling. We don't want to make each other out to be evil people. This is not—this is in a book it would be, but this is life. We all come with some broken suitcases. . . . What could you have done to pull her out of her pain?

BIRKHEAD: I just—I guess take all the drugs away, but I was told she needed them to live. So I didn't know if I took them, would she die or—had to choose, because they said, Howard told me that she could die . . .

But Larry Birkhead further testified that Howard did something else that stunned him during that hospital visit. Birkhead claims that at one point he caught Howard taking medication from his duffel bag and, unbeknownst to doctors, giving it directly to Anna, who felt the IV drip wasn't enough. Anna was there to kick her drug addiction, but he was only feeding her habit.

A month before this drug related testimony, unbeknownst to Howard K. Stern and Alex Goen, CEO of TrimSpa, one day in late January, Larry Birkhead met for several hours with seven Bahamian police detectives. Larry made some shocking allegations. The meeting was also attended and witnessed by fifty-two-year-old Mark Speer, a retired Los Angeles County sheriff's deputy, who was doing security for Larry Birkhead between October and March. He traveled with him everywhere including Florida, Los Angeles and the Bahamas, and saw first-hand some dramatic and very telling revelations.

During the meeting, Larry provided verbal and written statements with explosive details of money funneling, drug use and worse. Going on record, Larry Birkhead told police that Howard was funneling approximately $15,000 at least every other week, wiring it to his parents in offshore accounts. According to Larry, several million dollars had been wired. He said that Bahamian police should check Howard's bank accounts and Anna's checkbook.

But he also told police officers that "TrimSpa was a joke" and that "the owner, Alex Goen, knew Anna wouldn't and couldn't lose weight that way." So, he said, Goen supplied human growth hormone, a body fat reducer, and methamphetamines, an appetite suppressing, heart-racing stimulant often called "speed."

According to Mark Speer, Larry said he was "there when Alex Goen brought the stuff to Anna, and Anna also told Larry that this was going on." She said she had been using it for at least a year. Larry gave his attorney Debra Opri a two-to-three-inch-long needle and a vial with a small amount of liquid left in it. Debra Opri gave the items to Speer, who placed them in a sealed envelope in his refrigerator anticipating that they would be tested someday. Larry Birkhead said the needle came from

Alex Goen and that "The needle and the vial would have Anna's DNA and maybe Alex Goen's fingerprints." A few weeks later, after Larry had met privately with Howard, Larry asked Mark Speer for the envelope back. "This needle and this vial are going to take TrimSpa and Alex Goen down," Larry told Speer, adding that he wanted "Alex Goen to go to prison and his company out of business."

I asked Mark Speer why he thought Larry never did anything with this evidence. Very frankly he said, "I believe Larry Birkhead was bought off."

Birkhead had also told Bahamian police that he often saw Howard injecting Anna and that "Howard was stealing money from Anna, sending money to his parents and offshore banks in the amount of $15,000 every week or two weeks." Larry further said that millions of dollars were funneled from Anna's accounts to Howard's. "I saw Howard signing checks to himself and to Howard's banks in the States and offshore."

Speer told me that Larry's mission at the time was to get Howard arrested and convicted for the death of Daniel and the continued drugging of Anna Nicole. After his meeting, Bahamian police told Larry that this information would be very helpful with the inquest into Daniel's death, which was in their jurisdiction. "We'll need you to testify at the inquest," he was told, "as you'll be important to this case." Speer said by the way the officers were acting, "You could tell they felt the information was big."

But, according to Moe's statements to private investigators, Larry wasn't completely without fault when it came to drugs and Anna Nicole. Moe said, Larry is "no choir boy," in fact, he also joined the party, giving Anna drugs while she was pregnant. Moe said he's seen "Howard give her plenty of prescription drugs," but he also saw "Larry give Anna ecstacy and cocaine."

• • •

Though Larry Birkhead testified that he fought Anna about her drug use, his last fight, he said, with Anna was over a pair of sunglasses that he refused to buy her, showing how unpredictable she was. Ford Shelley, Ben Thompson's son-in-law, told me he knows about that fight, but Jackie Hatten says that Larry Birkhead and Anna had a much bigger blow-up over Anna finding out that Larry had sold a photo of her behind her back. As a photojournalist, this was, after all, what he did for a living, but Anna always wanted to be aware of what pictures were going where and who would get a cut of them.

According to Jackie, Anna wanted to get pregnant by Larry Birkhead so she could have a blonde-haired, blue-eyed baby. In a letter Anna had written her mother on March 3, 2000, Vickie said, "I want to get pregnant and have another baby before Daniel leaves me . . . I'll find someone just to get pregnant and not let him no [sic]. Is that so bad? I don't think so. Men are pigs." Larry may have fit the bill. She told Jackie that Larry was "cute, young, and not dangerous," but Jackie says, that after the photo incident, "She felt betrayed and taken advantage of."

"One thing that infuriated Anna was if anyone did any deals behind her back," Jackie said. "She always wanted to be the one brokering where the pictures would be sold, she always wanted to know about it. When she saw a picture in a magazine one day and knew it was one Larry took, but didn't tell her about selling, she went ballistic."

• • •

The dramatic court testimony of Anna Nicole Smith's abuse of prescription drugs culminated in the showing of a home video of a pregnant Anna in clown makeup pushing a baby carriage. Anna appeared drugged, silly, or as several commentators noted, "completely whacked out of her mind." Her bizarre behavior apparently frightened Riley, the nine-year-old granddaughter of Ben Thompson, who was visiting them in the Bahamas prior to the brouhaha over who owned the Horizons house. Riley had painted Anna's face to look like a clown.

HOWARD: Riley thinks you've absolutely lost your mind.

ANNA: Huh?

HOWARD: Riley thinks you've lost your mind.

ANNA: I didn't lose my mind.

HOWARD: She thinks you have.

ANNA: I didn't.

HOWARD: Is this a mushroom trip?

ANNA: Huh?

HOWARD: Is this a mushroom trip?

ANNA: What do you mean?

HOWARD: I'm kidding.

ANNA: What does that mean?

HOWARD: I'm kidding.

• • •

HOWARD: I said this footage is worth money.

ANNA: Why? What footage?

HOWARD: This thing you're looking into.

ANNA: That's a camera.

HOWARD: Exactly.

Howard was later infuriated that someone had stolen the video from the Horizons house soon after Anna died and released it to the media.

Meantime, while this circus of a courtroom scene was continuing, Dr. Perper, the coroner in charge of Anna's body, was getting nervous. It had been almost two weeks since Anna had died. He called the court several times from the Broward County morgue to report on the condition of the body. His words were being broadcast globally as many people were glued to their TV sets watching the daily courtroom theatrics. The body was, he said, rapidly decomposing and it was now a race against time. Dr. Perper told me he was shocked by the delay in the court proceedings and hoped his call would hasten the hearing that had now become must-see entertainment for millions of Americans.

The Will

During the hearing, there was discussion over Anna's will. Signed on July 30, 2001, the will was drafted by California attorney Eric Lund and was witnessed by Anna's purple-haired assistant, Kimberly Walther, and James Khavarian, a former law partner of Howard K. Stern's. Two days after signing the will, Khavarian was suspended for lying to a client and eventually he was disbarred.

It has been suggested that the first page of Anna's will has been newly inserted, indicated by a slightly different "VLM" initialing than on the other pages. In Article I on this first page, Anna states that she has "intentionally omitted to provide for my spouse and other heirs, including future spouses and children and other descendants now living or those hereafter born or adopted," except for Daniel.

In court, the will was presented to show Howard was nominated as the personal representative, but it was the other parts of the document that attracted unwanted attention.

On the top of the faxed copy of the will sent from Anna's attorney and Howard's good friend, Ron Rale, to Howard's Florida attorney, Krista Barth, it said "2/3 RAR" and "2:18 a.m." February 3—which would indicate that it was sent just five days before Anna died and several months after Daniel was already dead. Her will possibly being faxed five days before her death had tongues wagging outside and inside the courthouse. On the face of it, such an action would seem to be quite suspicious.

Meantime, legal experts differed over whether the will entitled Dannielynn to a share of Anna's estate since it oddly and expressly excluded children born after Daniel. Howard K. Stern's attorney, Krista Barth, did not think that part of the document pertained to the matter at hand. She told Judge Seidlin, "The will is presented to show that Mr. Stern is the nominated personal representative under the document."

"You—always want me to look at things in isolated ways," Judge Seidlin told her. "You take me to a museum and you tell me, 'Just look at this wall.' . . . 'Don't look at the other paintings . . . Just keep your eye on this one painting here.' How can I do this?"

KRISTA BARTH: Because the law recognizes the illegality of certain contracts. And most things in it have a severability clause. And I've reviewed it for that. But it says, most things say if one provision sells, the whole document doesn't sell.

JUDGE LARRY SEIDLIN: But you're now giving me contract law. And I respect that . . . . I'll tell you, it, it's when—a fish has a little smell, you get rid of the whole fish. This will is not just to take away a clause. You got to ask yourself, *"Did she read this will? Would any woman in America who read this will, sign this will? What state of mind was she in when she wrote the will?"*

But I'm telling you what I'm gonna do, though. I'm gonna tell you what I'm gonna do. It's a piece of evidence that'll be submitted to the court. And it'll, it has its holes in it, like we talked about. That balloon has plenty of holes in it, plenty of holes.

And one day, even to Bahamas or California, you'll try to admit it there. And then you, you let the chips fall as they may. I don't have the time to decide whether or not it's a valid will. It's a, it's a piece of paper that's purported to be a will that—causes me to lose more hair than I already lost. And you know it and I know it, because we can't fool each other. We're too good. We'll get a move on. You don't need to cross-examine this document anymore. We've done all the work for you.

Judge Seidlin pointed out what many were thinking—no woman in her right mind would ever sign a will that excludes her future children. But then he took Krista Barth's word that her fax machine in her office was messed up since she was claiming her daily office logs could confirm that the fax came after Anna died. But it seemed to go unnoticed that normally the time stamped on top of a fax is from the outgoing fax machine, not the incoming fax machine. The outgoing fax machine belonged to Ron Rale, Howard's long-time friend.

Even though Howard K. Stern admitted Anna was his only client, he testified that he doesn't really remember the will. When Judge Seidlin asked to see the original, attorney Krista Barth said they had their hands full and didn't have it. Though they did have time to get a written statement from Eric Lund, the will's drafter, to say he saw Anna sign it. Howard maintained he is not a beneficiary of the will.

KRISTA BARTH: She didn't leave you any money did she?

HOWARD K. STERN: Absolutely not.

BARTH: But she left you Daniel?

HOWARD: That is correct.

Howard K. Stern was listed as executor to oversee her estate and the affairs of Daniel, who was now dead. And Anna Nicole specifically excluded any future children from benefiting from her estate. Therefore, the executor, Howard K. Stern, would at his discretion determine how the funds of Anna's estate would be divided and utilized.

The Decision

On February 22, after enduring six days of weirdness and a body that had been chilling in the morgue for two weeks, Judge Seidlin surprised everyone—a day earlier than previously scheduled—and made his decision. My contacts in the Florida court system told me that Judge Seidlin had been called behind closed doors the day before and scolded by the chief judge. He was told to stop showboating and wrap it up as soon as he could.

"I have suffered for this," Seidlin announced, beginning to render his decision. "I have struggled with this, I have shed tears for your little girl." He turned to Virgie and choked up. "This is not a happy moment," he said, his voice cracking. "She's going to be with her son. She's going to have her son next to her."

Judge Seidlin ultimately left the decision of Smith's burial to court appointed guardian Richard Milstein, an attorney who specializes in guardianship, probate and mediation, and who was now the "guardian ad litem" of Anna Nicole Smith's five-month-old daughter. Seidlin then instructed Milstein to work with the three warring parties and the judge pleaded that they arrive at a decision for the burial that would be of mutual agreement. He told the packed courtroom that he hoped the former Playboy Playmate would be buried in the Bahamas next to her son Daniel.

"I want them to be together," he said.

Openly weeping, he urged all of the possible fathers of Smith's infant daughter to get a paternity test, and said, "I hope to God here that you two guys will give the kid the right shot." He then relinquished jurisdiction for the paternity and custody issues to another judge, and announced to the parties, "You're done with me. I'm prepared to handle any other tasks, but I've completed all my tasks in this case. Godspeed."

Virgie Arthur, Larry Birkhead, and Howard K. Stern all wiped away tears upon hearing the ruling.

Directly after the ruling, Judge Seidlin came over to Virgie Arthur and tried to put his arm around her, telling her, "I did the best I could."

Virgie pushed him away. She was enraged that this man, whom she later referred to as "a clown," had the audacity to say he'd done the best he could. "You kept talking about your six-year-old daughter in court," she said, seething. "One day she's going to have trouble and you're going to need help. Look at me. Look at my face. When you can't help her, remember my face."

• • •

Within less than an hour, Howard, Larry, and Virgie surprised the world by walking arm-in-arm outside the courthouse to hold a press conference to announce that the funeral would be in the Bahamas. Despite the show of solidarity, Virgie was visibly awkward. That night, when a secret meeting took place at Howard's hotel, The Riverside Hotel in Fort Lauderdale, Virgie Arthur was left out.

A driver took Ford Shelley, Larry Birkhead, and Mark Speer, Larry's security detail, to the hotel where they were greeted by Ron Rale and soon after Krista Barth, two of Howard's attorneys.

The attorneys left the room and the men talked for almost an hour. At first, Howard presented Ford and Larry with a confidentiality agreement to sign, saying that what they talked about could not be discussed. Both of them refused to sign the paper.

They ended up talking little about the funeral and instead listened a lot to Howard offering deals. When I saw Larry soon after the meeting, he told me Howard had said, "I want you to see your child." But then, Howard started dancing around it, saying "it could be your child or my child since Dannielynn came two weeks early." Ford Shelley repeated the same story and says it was clear in the conversation that Howard knew he wasn't the father. He says that Howard even floated the idea of bringing Dannielynn to Fort Lauderdale in a few days to get swabbed and tested, but it never happened.

When Debra Opri heard Howard was making such an offer, she knew he would never do it without Larry cutting a deal with him. Ford Shelley has said that Howard wanted them to drop all of their suits—Larry's paternity action and Ford and Ben Thompson's property action with the Horizons House—and settle out of court. "You could see Larry was desperate to see his child," Ford told me. "He wanted to see his child at whatever cost."

Though Ron Rale came out publicly saying that talks were happening, and they were trying to keep the lawyers out of it, Debra Opri made a statement that "Mr. Birkhead will not compromise his child for financial gain. There are absolutely no deals to get this child. The child will not be used as a financial pawn." She added, "If Stern was sincere about resolving this without lawyers, then he should simply appear with the baby and get the DNA test done."

On the drive home from that secret meeting, Mark Speer, who was in the car, overheard the discussions taking place between Larry Birkhead and Ford Shelley. They were talking about Howard's offer to Larry behind closed doors. The deal was if Larry agreed not to contest Howard remaining as executor of Anna's estate, then Larry could have his baby.

Mark Speer said later that he was surprised Larry seemed receptive to the idea. As conversations with Howard continued over the next few days, Howard sweetened the deal. If Larry agreed not to contest the will and allowed Howard to remain executor of Anna's estate as well as keep control of Anna's "name and likeness," Howard would:

- Drop all legal claims for custody of Dannielynn and "give you your baby."
- Allow Larry to "run the show" in California.
- Let Larry live in Anna's Studio City house. . . .
- Pay all the bills.
- Provide several thousand dollars a month in allowance . . . and pay for a rental car.

He also promised Larry that he would "take care of you the way I took care of Anna."

• • •

With word of all these offers, Debra Opri began arguing with her client, telling him not to talk to Howard. She felt that by his talking to the enemy of this litigation, he was allowing Howard to lure him in. She worried that since they were so close to getting a positive resolution in court without any side deals, Larry would be making a big mistake cutting a deal.

As they prepared for the funeral of Anna Nicole Smith, why was Larry going against both his family's wishes and those of his counsel?

What did Howard K. Stern have on Larry Birkhead?

CHAPTER 11

Rest in Peace

THERE WAS A HOLLYWOOD-STYLE RED CARPET—SUITABLE FOR premieres and award ceremonies—though Anna Nicole Smith wouldn't walk it and no one would get to see her pretty dress. Anna would make her last trip down the red carpet in a casket draped in a pink coverlet, adorned with feathers, ribbons and her big inimitable autograph in a trail of Swarovski crystals. The final embellishment on the coffin drape was a big smiley face, Anna's cute trademark in her famous signature.

Many onlookers from around the world gathered outside the church. The majority were Bahamian and American tourists. They watched the white hearse roll in, which was being escorted by three sheriff cars, a police van and five motorcycle police. They also bought snacks and sodas from vendors who had set up in the parking lots of the church and the adjacent shopping mall. Three helicopters hovered in the blue skies above the crowd, capturing aerial photos and video for media outlets around the globe.

With his balding pate shining in the hot sun, Richard Milstein, the court appointed guardian ad litem for Dannielynn, pontificated to those congregating outside the church, asking for "respect and solemnity." He told the crowd, "Today we share our grief with all of you. . . . Today we come to you to carry out the final, most sacred, solemn act provided to any individual.

"Unfortunately, in a time when life should have been reaching its highest peak for her, she received both a blessing and a curse," said Dannielynn's temporary guardian, the man that Anna Nicole never even knew. "She joyously gave birth to her only daughter, Dannielynn, and devastatingly, three days later, she lost her only son, Danny. If one were to write a Greek tragedy, one could not write a script as sorrowful and as hurtful as this."

Like a crowd at a Roman coliseum, the spectators, held behind steel barricades, booed and cheered as guests arrived at the white columned church. Walking into the church, attendees were judged by the crowd on an unwritten set of parameters and given either a cheering thumbs-up or a jeering thumbs-down. It was a fittingly inappropriate scene for the finale of the Anna Nicole Show.

But overall the Bahamian people themselves could not have been more gracious and endearing to their visiting guests. Many Bahamian citizens and reporters wanted to make sure their island was portrayed in the best and fullest light possible, not just by the Anna Nicole Smith saga. Fearful of becoming "another Aruba," a reference to the unsolved Natalee Holloway case, islanders were worried about how the story might affect tourism on their idyllic vacation spot. Officials handled it as best they could. There was no way they could have foreseen the crush of people who would surround every event even remotely related to Anna Nicole.

In fact, a few days before the funeral, when I was interviewing Virgie Arthur outside the main downtown courthouse in Nassau among a pack of many other reporters and cameras, the scene turned into sheer bedlam. With no crowd control to protect her from the voracious media and onlookers, a mob scene overtook Anna Nicole's mother. The horde swarmed around her, packed in like sardines, trying to get any words from Anna Nicole's mother. It became so crowded and chaotic that my feet were literally not even touching the ground for a few seconds. There were spectators climbing on top of her limousine just to take a quick picture, just to get a glimpse.

It had been a week not just of in-your-face maneuvering by the media, but also of a lot of behind-the-scenes negotiations among the interested parties. Howard K. Stern had been privately floating the idea to Ford Shelley that he would give up Anna's new boat and her new yet to be lived in waterfront home in Nassau in exchange for keeping "Horizons," the house in which Howard was currently living and the one Ben and Ford were trying to kick him out of.

The night before the funeral, Howard presented Larry with a contract and tried "strong-arming" him into signing a $250,000 deal with *Entertainment Tonight*. The arrangement gave the media outlet sole access to the funeral with the proceeds supposedly going to a trust fund for little Dannielynn. Several people involved feared that even if *Entertainment Tonight* had good intentions, the parties were wary the money might not end up where Howard claimed, or he would cut a separate deal on the side.

According to sources close to the case, Richard Milstein himself was sending around the contract to the parties. Both Virgie's and Larry Birkhead's legal teams were suspicious of Howard and, by now, also Milstein. Neither Virgie nor Larry wanted to sign the document. Milstein told the parties he also didn't want to be the one to have to sign it, leading some to think that he didn't want to get his hands dirty with any media related deal. The parties found it ironic that he personally was circulating this deal, given that he had slammed everyone in the Florida courtroom for accepting anything from the media—whether it be money, a flight, or a free hotel.

Each of the parties worried that it would look bad to sign any media deal on the eve of Anna's funeral. But in the end, *Entertainment Tonight* had the only video cameras inside. Though Milstein had been visibly cold to Howard K. Stern during the Florida trial, by the funeral they seemed like old chums. During the service, Richard Milstein sat next to Mark Steines, co-anchor of *Entertainment Tonight*.

Mount Horeb Baptist Church, March 2, 2007, Nassau, Bahamas

Virgie Arthur had invited me to be her guest at the funeral, and I didn't realize until I got there that I was the *only* on-air member of the press allowed inside, besides the crew of *Entertainment Tonight*. But when I arrived at the bottom of the church steps, I soon discovered my name was not on "the list." Though my producer's name, unrecognizable to Howard K. Stern, had been successfully included, my name was mysteriously missing.

Ford Shelley and his family were also supposed to go to

the funeral, but were told by Howard the night before that he changed his mind. Howard said the church was full, which was far from the truth. After the secret meeting in Howard's hotel room in Florida, Howard was arguing again with Ben Thompson and Ford Shelley over who owned the house, which Howard wanted to now desperately keep, even if it was only to save face with the public. Howard had in fact told Ford that he had contacts with certain Bahamian officials and Ford might be arrested if he dared step into the Bahamas. Ford was worried his family would be in danger if he came to the island, and didn't push it, therefore missing his chance to bid his final farewell to a dear friend.

Fortunately, I was allowed to enter by the funeral official at the door, who said he knew I had been invited, as he overheard many discussions about it. He told me to enter the church and that we'd "figure it out inside." I didn't find out until later that Milstein and Howard K. Stern's attorneys had tried feverishly to remove my name, only to be overridden by the other parties who stated that the funeral should not be closed off to people they trust. I also later discovered that as part of the carefully negotiated funeral "deal," the various authorized parties agreed that two of them (of Howard, Virgie, and Larry) had to strike a name from the list in order for that person's invitation to be rescinded. Larry told me that Howard pleaded with him to strike my name, as Howard wanted *Entertainment Tonight* to have the "exclusive," but Larry insisted on keeping me on the list. And Virgie was not budging at all.

I waited in the back of the church, and from that vantage point immediately noticed the disparity in the size of the crowd on either side of the room. The pews on the right, Howard's side, were quite full, including where they placed Larry Birkhead, Richard Milstein, and their guests. Only a handful

of people sat on the left, Virgie's side, which included Dr. Perper and two others, one of them my producer. Howard, as I
discovered, had convinced Larry to relinquish 45 of his 50 allotted seats so that Howard could accommodate all his guests
on one side. Howard had 95 seats; Larry had 5. It was supposed to have been 50/50.

"Anna would have wanted a huge funeral," Jackie Hatten
said. "And she would have never wanted one in a foreign
country where all her friends and fans couldn't go and where
she didn't know anyone very well. She also would have
wanted to be buried in an all-white casket with pink satin
inside. . . . Why was there a brown casket and closed services
if Howard was really doing what Anna wanted? If that was
really the goal."

Peter Nygard agrees. "Anna would have wanted to lie in
state," he told me. "She would have wanted people walking
by that casket for days."

At the funeral I was privy to several interesting conversations, including learning that Dr. Perper told Dr. Khris Eroshevich, "What you told me was very useful" and thanking
her for her cooperation in helping him reach his conclusions.

I was also thrust into making a decision that I never imagined. The funeral was supposed to begin, and Anna's mother
Virgie was still nowhere to be found. Virgie's delay made the
situation in the back of the church noticeably uncomfortable
and tense. Howard wanted to start, and start now. His people
were beginning to make a ruckus with the funeral directors.
Patrik Simpson, one of Howard's most vocal defenders and
friend, was loudly asking, "Where's the bitch? Where's that
bitch? Let the funeral go on without the bitch," referring to
Virgie who still had not shown up. I overheard people close to
Howard celebrating Virgie's absence, going so far as to say

how good Howard was going to look in the press, if Virgie missed her own daughter's funeral.

David Giancola, the director of *Illegal Aliens*, Anna's last film, told me, he was infuriated that Virgie made them sit in church and wait while Anna's body sat outside in a hearse. "Let's get her body and hijack it," he told several of Howard's friends.

Anna's friend designer Pol Atteu and others said that was a bad idea, responding, "It's surrounded by Bahamian police."

"Well," David Giancola said. "Anna wants to get buried."

Ron Rale, who officially broke the news with me on air that Anna had died, came over and asked me if I knew where Virgie was or if she was even coming. He said he had heard some buzz that Anna Nicole's mother was trying to stop the burial.

In fact, I knew where Virgie Arthur was. Virgie was at the Bahamian courthouse filing a last minute petition to put a stop to the burial. As her daughter's body lay inside a mahogany coffin in the back of a hearse parked in the hot Bahamian sun, Virgie and her attorneys were appealing to Justice Anita Allen to have Anna's body sent back to the United States.

I stalled Ron Rale with a few questions, and then told him what I knew and had already reported publicly on the air. He ran to the front right side of the church (Howard's side) where I watched him tell Howard the news as he sat in the front pew. Ron then returned to the back of the church and asked me questions about the filing. Seeing this as an opportunity to talk face to face with Howard, I smiled and said, "If Howard wants to know, why don't you have him come back here and talk to me himself." Ron walked to the front, whispered in Howard's ear, and Howard sauntered to the back of the church, wearing ribbons of black and pink on his lapel.

Meekly he asked, "When is she getting here? We can't keep holding this thing up." I said I didn't know, that I thought she was only a few minutes away. I truly did not know how long the hold up would be, but thought she was on her way. He then said in a huff, "We're going to set a deadline. We're not waiting." He turned to Ron Rale and gave a nod.

"Wheels up, boys," Ron Rale said to the funeral directors. "Let's get this show on the road."

One of the funeral directors then came over to me and whispered, "What do you think I should do? They want this to go on without her?"

"This is only going to happen once," I said. "It would be really sad if a mother missed her own daughter's funeral." He agreed and told me he was going to try to come up with some excuse to stall the increasingly loud clamoring from Howard and his people.

Once Virgie's courthouse pleas had fallen on deaf ears, she had gotten caught up in the traffic jam created by the highest-profile funeral the Bahamas has ever seen. When Virgie Arthur finally arrived at her daughter's funeral in a white stretch limousine, Patrik Simpson loudly announced to those of us standing in the back of the church, "The bitch is here!" But that was minor compared to what she herself heard outside.

The crowd greeted Virgie Arthur with a resounding and loud chorus of thumbs down jeers. Virgie told me later, "It was the worst feeling in the world." But she said she knew Anna would want her to fight to the bitter end. "I know my daughter was supporting me as I walked into the church, even though no one else was," she said. When she was greeted by hundreds and hundreds of people booing her, she said, "Every step my feet felt like they weighed fifty pounds. I kept saying to myself, 'there's not much further,' but it felt like a mile as I walked to that church."

She walked down the aisle and took her seat in the pew across the aisle from Howard, only a few feet in front of me. I had positioned myself on the aisle so that I could have a good view of all parties. The tension between the two sides of the church was palpable. Howard's crowd glared at her from across the aisle in utter disgust.

•   •   •

It had already been a long day for those traveling with Anna Nicole to her final resting place. Anna Nicole's body had been picked up at the Broward County Medical Examiner's office in Fort Lauderdale in the wee hours of the morning and driven to Miami International Airport, surrounded by a long line of cars and police protection. It was put on a private plane and flown to the Bahamas under the watchful eye of Dr. Joshua Perper and bodyguard Moe Brighthaupt, protecting her in death as he had tried to do in life. After they landed at the Million Air Airport in Nassau, a motorcade had transported Anna's casket to the Mount Horeb Church in a white hearse. It and Anna's body had been waiting for more than two hours for its cue, since it arrived early for the service, which ended up starting forty minutes late due to Virgie's last-ditch legal delay.

When the casket finally came into the church, it was a somber, powerful moment. It was carried down the aisle by Anna's pallbearers, which included Ron Rale, Moe, and two of Anna's other ex-bodyguards. She was placed in the front of the church beneath the giant cathedral ceiling and large stained glass window, which sunlight streamed through. Anna Nicole, surrounded by pink flowers and two large photos of herself, was wearing a tiara and a specially designed, beaded gown by Pol

Atteu, who had designed more than a dozen gowns for her over the years, including the black dress and veil she had worn to bury Daniel only a few months before. But besides the casket's pink drape, Pol Atteu's work would today remain unseen inside the closed casket.

Anna Nicole Smith's body was now three weeks into death.

• • •

Anna Nicole's funeral on March 2, 2007, at Mount Horeb Baptist Church was a mix of the religious with the "over-the-top." The Reverend Dr. Lloyd Smith opened the service: "We brought nothing into this world and we take nothing out. The Lord giveth and the Lord taketh away."

The congregation, all wearing pink and black ribbons, numbered barely more than a hundred, including TrimSpa CEO Alex Goen, ex-assistant Kim Walther, and Slash from Guns N' Roses, who told me after the service that he met Anna at an event years before. Noticeably absent were Shane Gibson, the former Immigration Minister who resigned after the scandalous photos of him and Anna hit the front page of the local newspaper, and Dannielynn.

Before the funeral, Larry Birkhead told Howard repeatedly on the phone that he did not want the baby there. According to Mark Speer, Larry's security detail, "Larry was worried Howard would pass the baby to him" and get a photo taken. Then, he'd "sell it and make big money." Since no one had a photo yet of Larry and the baby together, Larry figured, "Howard will make another million if he gets the first shot of me and my baby. That's worth at least one million dollars right away, and probably another million more until she's eighteen." Then, he spoke like a true paparazzi: "That's my shot."

Anna's dead husband, oil tycoon J. Howard Marshall, made an unannounced appearance at the funeral. Half of Marshall's ashes had been awarded to Anna during her legal battle for his estate. After his sometimes "guest starring" role in the urn on the *Anna Nicole Show*, for the funeral he was carried in his urn by Moe and would later be placed in the coffin beside Vickie Lynn Marshall, his wife.

As former Bahamian senator Ruby Ann Darling played the organ, the congregation joined in the song, "What a Friend We Have in Jesus," followed by "Amazing Grace." After the minister's scripture reading, Virgie spoke first. Days earlier, both she and Larry Birkhead had individually asked me if I thought that they should speak at all and, if they did, my thoughts on what they should say. I told them both to speak from the heart and perhaps about the great things they deeply felt about Anna and their special memories. When they stood behind the pulpit, they both eloquently and emotionally discussed their relationship with Anna as well as her relationship with everyone in the room. Virgie sobbed through most of her eulogy.

"I was there when God gave you to me," Virgie began her eulogy. "You were a beautiful baby, you were so loved. . . . We all loved you and have so many stories to tell about you."

As she wiped tears away, the mother who had not physically seen her daughter in over a decade continued, "We watched you grow into a beautiful woman and we watched you stumble a few times—but you always got back up and carried on. . . . So headstrong, you accomplished all of the wonderful dreams that you wanted."

Anna's mother ended her memorial speech with, "We love you and know that you loved us. Goodbye, my baby daughter." She softly touched the casket and wept.

Larry Birkhead focused on Anna's small-town side—one not

as apparent to the public. "Anna Nicole could often be misunderstood," he said. "Misunderstood on what she wanted from life and what she needed. If Anna Nicole was guilty of one thing, it was that she wanted each and every one of us to feel like we were the most important in her world and number one."

Birkhead, obviously emotional, noted the humble side of Anna by describing a scenario where she took little hotel ketchup packets and put them into her suitcase. He said they represented security, "a security for Anna Nicole in a world that often seemed uncertain."

Larry and Virgie did not focus on any of the legal fights. They stayed positive and focused on Anna. Larry ended his eulogy with the line he used to say to her every night before she went to bed: "Good night, sweet Anna baby." After he sat back in the pew, he broke down and sobbed.

Country singer Joe Nichols sang two songs during the service. Anna met Joe Nichols at the Grand Ole Opry in 2005 and had become a big fan of his music. Howard had requested he sing, "I'll Wait for You" and Dolly Parton's "Wings of a Dove," which is said to have been Anna's favorite country song.

After Nichols finished this emotional and hopeful song, Howard K. Stern got up and unexpectedly used the pulpit like a lawyer in a courtroom, delivering an impassioned closing argument more than a sentimental eulogy.

"The truth . . . there's only one truth," he began. "And it's not what people say in court, even if those people are your blood relatives." He spoke the words glaring directly at Virgie Arthur. "It's not what people who claim to be your friends say to the media. . . . The truth is . . . what you touch, what you feel, what you see with your own eyes, what you observe for yourself. I know the truth about Anna. . . . She controlled her life . . . and her judgment wasn't clouded by anything.

"I can't believe that you're gone and you're not here to protect anyone," he said. "Sometimes I don't know how I'm gonna go on, but I know that my work isn't done. I still have to protect you, I have to protect your wishes, I have to protect your name, and most of all I have to protect Dannielynn, and I promise you, as long as I'm still breathing, I will, no matter who comes at me.

"You and I, we know the truth. We lived it."

When he finished, the right side of the congregation broke into raucous applause and gave him a standing ovation. The left side was stunned. Howard gently kissed Anna's casket and took his seat.

Director David Giancola was one of the first to stand up and applaud after Howard spoke. "I knew Anna didn't like her mom," David told me. "There was so much rage for her mom after Daniel's death because of what Virgie said on TV. I remember the Reverend asked the crowd, 'Where's the humanity here? What's wrong with you?'

"When Howard spoke, he said everything I felt too at that moment," Giancola said. "It was spontaneous and emotional and I hated her too."

• • •

Howard also clearly hated Debra Opri, his adversary in the paternity litigation. She was someone he knew he couldn't win over. She wasn't willing to cut any backdoor deals. And Larry knew of Howard's disdain for Opri, which is perhaps why, at the reception after the funeral, an unusual conversation took place.

The post funeral reception was held at a multi-million dollar home in the Ocean Club Estates, an exclusive gated community in the most luxurius part of Nassau. The house was filled with hundreds of guests who mingled both inside and outside the spacious home and grounds.

A most unusual conversation was overheard at this party by Larry's security detail, Mark Speer, shortly before my arrival at the event. Mark Speer noted that Howard and Larry gave each other a big hug, and Larry apologized to Howard for bringing Debra Opri to the funeral, even though Howard had for days been trying to convince him not to let her go. Opri had insisted, saying "I'm not going to let you be there by yourself, especially with Howard."

Larry told Howard, "I'm sorry I had to bring her. It just wouldn't look right if I didn't have anybody there."

Howard responded, "I understand, we'll get past it."

And then, in a remark that didn't sit well with Mark Speer, Howard told Larry "We'll take care of Debra later."

I arrived at the reception late, after I finished my reports about the funeral and ran the taped interview I conducted after the service with Larry Birkhead. I found out later that Larry and his attorney Debra Opri had left shortly before my arrival when they heard Howard's attorney, Krista Barth, was about to arrive. They didn't want any drama, and knew that Krista Barth's presence was sure to cause problems for them.

I had said on-air that Howard's eulogy was "surprising," and that "it was a very strange, sort of surreal moment" that many felt was inappropriate. Krista Barth did not like to hear any even partially negative comments about Howard and she was on the attack. Soon after I arrived at the reception, she sought me out. Even though I was personally invited by the owner of the home, she tried to get Bahamian police to remove me from the premises, which fell on deaf ears. When that failed, Ron Rale and I went to talk in a private room and were soon joined by Krista Barth and my producer. We had a very frank discussion in which Barth told me she thought it was inappropriate the way I had described on television "Howard's loving, tender, heartfelt eulogy."

I was stunned that she used those words to describe his angry tirade, and I told her that others had had the same sentiments of his words as I did. I also personally felt that my comments were quite "diplomatic." I told her my job was "to present what I saw, not to do P.R. for Howard K. Stern." I reminded her that I had done some favorable stories about Howard recently and that my responsibility was to present the facts.

"How'd you even get to go to the funeral anyway?" she demanded. "I wasn't even going to the funeral."

"I was invited," I laughed. "You should get better connections."

She didn't think that was funny. "I can't believe you'd go as a guest of Virgie's," she countered. "Yuck! We hate Virgie. She's the enemy."

I explained if Howard had invited me I'd have gone as his guest too, that any journalist would have seized the opportunity to be inside that church. She then asked me, how I had gotten into this party. "Howard didn't invite you." When I told her I had been invited by the actual owner of the house, she seemed surprised, but said, "Well, it's Howard's party, so maybe you should leave."

I told Krista Barth that I was planning on leaving soon anyway, but would take my time as I was going to talk to a few people before I left, including the person who, again, actually threw the party. I did just that, and gave several people a friendly goodbye before heading out. Days later, *Entertainment Tonight* spun a story about my crashing the party, which I found hilarious. The owner of the house, Shery Oakes, told me that she was furious when she saw the story on television as she had told Howard's team my "coverage was always fair and Rita was absolutely my invited guest." She said they apologized to her and she insisted they apologize to me. She was surprised to find out that months later they still had not. "I think they were upset you sat with Virgie's side," she said. "Which is ridiculous, total nonsense."

Lakeview Memorial Gardens, John F. Kennedy Drive, Nassau

At the private graveside service after the funeral, mourners were each handed a red rose and a pink rose to place on the coffin. The red rose symbolized Daniel, while the pink symbolized Anna. Mother and son would now be reunited, side-by-side for eternity. Well, maybe for eternity. Just hours before, Billy Smith, Daniel's father and Anna's estranged ex-husband, filed a petition in the Bahamian Supreme Court to have Daniel's body exhumed, hoping that if he was victorious in that filing and based on Anna's desire to be by her son, her exhumation could soon follow.

Each guest at Anna's graveside service was asked to write a personal note to Anna on pink heart shaped paper. The messages were dropped into the grave so her casket would be engulfed in messages of love. As a final act, a dozen white doves were released signifying "peace." One of the doves came to rest on top of Anna Nicole Smith's coffin, even as it was being lowered into the ground.

At the church, Howard and his team had been so mad at Virgie for holding up things that they wouldn't let Virgie's son be one of the pallbearers and even refused to let Virgie put out any of her family photographs. At the gravesite, however,

Virgie Arthur made a surprise addition to the many roses that mourners placed atop Anna's mahogany coffin—an 8x10 photo of herself kissing her daughter.

The ceremonial shoveling of dirt onto Anna's pink-covered coffin commenced with Howard scooping dirt out of the back of a truck onto the lowered coffin, then Howard's friend Ron Rale, followed by Anna's bodyguard Moe. In a move that was by some accounts as extreme as the entire funeral itself, Anna Nicole's mother, Virgie Arthur, asked to go last. She walked to the grave, threw the photo of her and Anna on the coffin, and quickly picked up the shovel. Howard seemed noticeably displeased with this unannounced action. But what could he do? He couldn't reach down and pull it out.

There was no stopping Virgie. She was going to make sure they weren't able to retrieve the picture. She began shoveling mound after mound of dirt into the grave. "I brought you into this world," Virgie remembers thinking, "and I'm going to be the last to send you out." She zealously shoveled for a full two minutes, dumping fifty-one shovelfuls of dirt onto her daughter's mahogany coffin. In spite of everything, Virgie Arthur is happy that the photo of her and Anna was forever laid to rest atop her daughter's casket.

CHAPTER 12

DNA

IT WAS ON THE WAY BACK FROM THE BURIAL THAT LARRY BIRK-head stopped at his Bahamian attorney's office so that he could privately sign the one million dollar media contract that his attorney, Debra Opri, had secured for him. The monies went into a client trust account at Opri's law firm. Typically, such trust accounts are kept to prevent commingling of client fees received by attorneys. Larry contended that this payment was not for legal fees and should have gone directly to him. Their relationship began to sour. Larry Birkhead and Debra Opri ended up in a lawsuit of their own over her fees and their media agreement.

After receiving her $620,492.84 bill, Larry Birkhead not only said he wasn't going to pay it, he filed a $885,000 suit against her alleging legal malpractice, saying she defrauded him out of hundreds of thousands of dollars, as well as seeking punitive remuneration. In his lawsuit, Larry claimed that her $620,492.84 bill was excessive and said the deal they reached stated that Opri would work for free because she knew the publicity generated by the case would be good for her visibility. In her response, Opri says it's a case of a client not living up to his obligation, and her retainer agreement signed by Larry Birkhead proves it.

Debra Opri also says that Larry Birkhead isn't the sweet guy that he had America believing. Yes, he wanted his daughter, but he also wanted his time in the media spotlight and the monies that attention would bring him. She has two fee agreements with Larry Birkhead: one an hourly rate for legal fees and a separate agreement under which she would get a commission/percentage for media deals. She contends that as a result of the second agreement, the money for the media deal was appropriately placed in his client trust account.

I was unaware of the terms of either deal, and have never received confidential documents from Debra Opri. I also have never been given any interviews as payback for referring him to her, as he alleged in his filing. In fact, Larry Birkhead and I were discussing many details of his case and setting up an interview, before Opri ever got involved.

What Opri says in her response filing is that when Larry came to her it seems he was very concerned about his public image. She says both Howard K. Stern and Anna Nicole had been characterizing him to the media as a "freeloading wannabe famous person, who was in reality a loser 'surfer boy' paparazzi." He wanted to become popular "like a sex symbol" so that people would support him and he would develop a "following," so that he could eventually have his own media career.

In her response, Debra Opri said their goal was to establish him as a shy and quiet, "aw shucks nice guy." She says it was a deliberate decision at first to keep Larry from speaking in court and quiet during most press conferences because "his silence created an image of someone who was there for no other reason than he wanted his attorney to fight for his child." And, she says, the nice guy image worked. America embraced him. But behind the scenes, she says, was a different story. "Birkhead was demanding, and threw temper tantrums regularly." And after Anna died, his "behavior became even more extreme."

Prior to the Florida hearings regarding where Anna's remains would be buried and who should have control of them, Larry Birkhead had originally agreed with his attorney's assessment that "it wasn't their fight," that they "didn't belong in Florida," that this battle was "between Virgie and Howard."

When the hearings started, eight days after Anna's death, Opri filed a motion in California requesting that the court order that Anna's DNA be preserved for testing. The court granted her motion, subject to Florida's consent. Her filing says, "Accordingly, Opri now had to secure Florida counsel to secure enforcement of this order so that Anna's DNA could be protected for paternity testing."

In the middle of February, when Judge Seidlin announced that he would be taking statements as to Anna's "intent," Larry Birkhead changed his mind and instructed Opri to tell the court that he "would appear in person" that he "had information that he wanted to testify to." Larry told Opri that Florida was "where all the action" was and that he wanted to be a part of the big "photo op."

In Florida, while staying as guests at a friend's 14,000 square foot home in Fort Lauderdale, he had Opri shop for (and put on her credit cards) outfits, including sunglasses for him to wear for his court appearances. In addition, rather than the inexpensive rental car his attorney had suggested, he instead asked her to pay for a daily private car and driver on his behalf. He said he wanted to arrive at court each day the "same way as Howard," who arrived each morning in a black SUV with a driver.

According to her court papers, Larry's behavior changed drastically after the Florida hearings, most noticeably after he had the "secret" meeting with Howard, which Opri reluctantly allowed him to do. During that meeting, "Birkhead was asked to come to an arrangement with Stern in return for him 'not challenging the paternity anymore.'" Opri claims that Ford Shelley leaked the meeting to the press to create tension between Opri and Larry and the present public appearance that Larry was beginning to distance himself from his lawyer and do his own deal. "The conduct from thereon, by Stern and his attorneys," Opri charges, "was clearly to show the media that Birkhead would be better off without Opri. Birkhead, while telling Opri in private that this was not happening, actually started dealing directly with Stern concerning all aspects of the case, such that Stern and his lawyers knew everything that Opri was doing in her case, thanks to Birkhead." Opri felt she had a runaway client.

During the secret meeting Howard and Larry had in Florida, Larry had been promised he'd get to meet his daughter for the first time, after seeing her for months, only through pictures shown on television. When he arrived in the Bahamas days before the funeral of Anna Nicole, he was granted a visit with little Dannielynn. Mark Speer, Larry Birkhead's security guard, was at the Horizons house, a few feet from where Larry and Howard had their discussion and saw and heard virtually every detail. He thought it was odd that Judy Birkhead, Larry's sister, walked in and barely acknowledged Howard. But Larry and Howard gave each other a big "full-armed embrace" as soon as Larry walked in the door. "It seemed like a familiar embrace," Speer told me. "It wasn't an awkward moment in any way. It stunned me."

Howard presented Dannielynn and said, "Here's your baby." But for the entire forty-five minute visit, Larry was forced to use a towel to keep her mouth from touching his clothing or skin. At one point, the baby spit up on the towel and Howard said, "I bet you'd like to have this towel" as he took it away. Howard wanted no DNA evidence on Larry's body when he left. They were, after all, still in the middle of a bitter paternity suit, despite the unusual embrace.

Mark Speer heard first hand Howard's proposal to Larry: "I will give you your baby, if you leave me as executor of the estate." Speer, a retired deputy sheriff later told me, "I felt like arresting Howard then and there for kidnapping and holding the baby for ransom. If I could have."

Larry responded to Howard: "I'm not going to leave you as executor."

Howard then said to Larry: "It only makes sense if I keep running her business. I'll also pay you an on-going fee."

"You don't have to pay me a fee," Larry said. "Because whatever's there is mine anyway. This is not going to happen."

Speer told me he "thought this was strange for Larry to say because Dannielynn would inherit Anna's estate, not Larry Birkhead."

Despite Larry's reticence at the house, what seemed like an astonishing alliance was beginning to form. Larry spoke incessantly to Howard K. Stern throughout the day and well into the night. Opri felt her client was being used by Howard and coerced into a deal he didn't have to make. She thought Birkhead would win in the courts and legitimately get his baby in a matter of weeks. Opri believed Howard knew this too and was using every bargaining chip in his arsenal as well as playing on Larry's strong and immediate desire to get his baby in order to rush and strike a deal.

Larry was also beginning to seek Howard's advice. "He would be on the phone with Howard while he sat in his hotel room surfing the internet to see how many photos/stories of him had made it into the media that day," Opri charges. "If a story did not sound favorable to him, he would call Stern to ask what he should do."

Mark Speer told me he loaned Larry his cell phone during this time period, resulting in two phone bills totaling $3100, which normally averaged $150 a month in usage. Larry kept promising to pay Speer back, but never did. Meanwhile, Larry's family urged him to listen to his attorney's advice and though he told them "Yeah, yeah, yeah," he'd immediately get right back on the phone with Howard K. Stern. "I warned him as a law enforcement officer to be careful," Speer said. "I told him, 'he's clearly trapping you.'"

Opri says she "told Birkhead that he was in over his head with Stern, and that, like Anna, Stern was 'reeling him in.'" While the funeral arrangements were being made, Opri overheard many conversations between Howard and Larry; most of the conversations had nothing to do with burial plans.

Before the funeral, a Bahamian judge stated that Virgie should be allowed to see her granddaughter, so upon the court's direction, Virgie went to Horizons. During her visit, which only lasted about twenty-five minutes, tension was very thick between her and Howard. When she went to touch the baby, Howard stopped her. "No," he said. "The judge said you could *see* her, not *touch* her." But, again, Howard offered another Dannielynn deal. "If you let Vickie be buried in the Bahamas, I'll let you hold her and kiss her." Virgie would not agree to drop her last minute legal actions and left the house without ever touching her beautiful little granddaughter.

During that same trip to the Bahamas, Virgie met with Larry at the Hilton Hotel. She told him in her Texas drawl, "I believe in you, son. You seem like a good, decent guy. I believe you are the baby's father, and I will help you in any way I can against Howard."

Virgie thought she and Larry got along well and had developed an understanding, and a great partnership. Within weeks, she would realize that she was sadly mistaken.

At one point in the Bahamas, Debra Opri and Larry Birkhead had a big fight because she caught him on the phone again with Howard. "They were not talking about funeral arrangements," Opri charges. "But rather what Birkhead would have to do to get his child, including 'ending all litigation against Stern and not testifying against him in the inquest.'" This infuriated Opri. She asked Larry, "What exactly is going on between the two of you?" She told him, "He's the enemy in this litigation, and until he agrees to a DNA test for Dannielynn, you can't talk to him about this case." Though Larry promised he would not speak to Howard anymore, minutes later he was back on the phone with Howard K. Stern.

I had been with Larry walking around the shops of the Atlantis Hotel a few nights before he left. He was looking at baby things. He was buying clothes, rattles, and stuffed animals so that he could take them over to Dannielynn before he left back to the States. But Howard would not allow Larry to see the baby again when he went to drop off the items before he left the Bahamas. Though Larry begged Howard to let him see the baby for a second time, Howard said, "You can't. You haven't done anything for me."

Hours later, Larry left on the plane for home. He was sobbing and desperate to see his child.

Soon after this Virgie says everything suddenly changed and she found herself completely cut out. Howard, who had deprived Larry of seeing his daughter for months, and had put him through a costly legal battle, abruptly dropped all challenges to the custody, clearing the way for an immediate DNA test. Remarkably, he removed the hurdles he'd been putting up for months. "Suddenly Howard has essentially become his advisor," an investigator for Virgie told me. "It just doesn't make sense . . . . Larry had all the cards, he didn't need to fold to Howard."

Virgie told me that she wishes all the money tied to Anna's billionaire late husband was gone. She suggested in court that a trust be set up with several people overseeing any funds the baby might receive at some point. She wanted people such as Larry's own parents and herself reviewing this trust. Larry quickly declined this offer. "I believe the dollars are tainted," she told me. "And I don't believe Larry's shown he's responsible enough to manage the baby's affairs with Howard Stern by his side." Judge Seidlin's words that "money was the root of all evil" echoed in my head.

At the Hilton Hotel the day that Virgie and Larry had met, Virgie says she had an eye-opening conversation with a desperate and nervous young man. Virgie asked Larry Birkhead about Howard. "What does he have on you?"

"They have so much stuff on me," Larry told her.

"Son, what kind of stuff?" Virgie asked.

"They're fixing to tell all about me," he said. "They say they caught me dating other men. That I'm queer."

"What do they have?" Virgie asked. "Do they have a tape?"

"I'm tired . . . " Larry said, "and I just want to take my daughter home."

"I don't care if you have men, women, farm animals in your life. If you are the baby's daddy, and I believe you are, it doesn't matter what they say, I will stand by you, son, one hundred percent."

Larry paused and took a deep breath, then he told her, "All I want to do is take my daughter and go home."

What Howard knew about Larry was something Larry didn't want the world—but perhaps more importantly his devout Southern Baptist family—to find out. It is his skeleton in the closet. And, like others involved in this sordid tale, it is often these kept secrets that make people act in ways and do things that they normally would not do.

• • •

One of Anna's closest friends, Jackie Hatten, says she knows what Howard has on Larry.

One night at a friend's house in Los Angeles, Jackie was supposed to meet Larry Birkhead for the first time. Anna had been telling her about the blond-haired, blue-eyed photographer that she'd been seeing, and wanted her to meet him. Late that night at the party, Jackie went looking for Anna around the house. Jackie walked down a hallway, peaking into rooms. In one darkened bedroom, she came upon two men—Howard K. Stern and another man, whom she was about to discover, was Anna's boyfriend, Larry Birkhead.

She says both men had their shirts off and Howard was down on his knees. Larry was sitting in a big oversized loveseat chair and both men had their pants down around their ankles. "Howard's head was down into Larry's crotch," Jackie told me. "Their bodies were intermingled. It was obvious what was happening." Anna suddenly walked up behind her and laughed out loud when she also saw what the two men were doing.

"The boys didn't stop," Jackie said. "They were engrossed and making their own sounds." Jackie said she and Anna watched the scene from about fifteen feet away. "Definitely close enough to see what was happening."

Jackie was shocked. Anna wasn't. She grabbed her friend's arm. "Come here, come here, come here," Anna said. "Howard . . . you know he's gay, I told you. And if Larry wants to do it, I can't complain because I do, what I do." Anna's sexual escapades with women were openly discussed between she and her friends. "I guess anything goes," Anna had laughed.

Several former boyfriends told me that Anna preferred women to men. "She was like Mae West with men," one told me. "She loved the attention of men constantly, but privately loved women." He recounted to me that one night when she was in a hot tub at his house during a big party, eight women between the ages of twenty and thirty years old who didn't know Anna before that night, joined her in the water. "They all got naked and began touching her and each other," he said. "The night became very spontaneous and it went from the Jacuzzi to a private suite and it went on all night long." It was one time of many. "She constantly had an interest in women."

The following day after the Howard and Larry man-on-man shenanigans, Jackie and Anna talked about what they had seen in the bedroom at their friend's house. "Oh, you were freaked out about last night," Anna giggled.

"I wasn't expecting to see that!" Jackie said. Anna laughed and laughed. She thought it was the funniest thing ever that the night Jackie was supposed to meet Anna's boyfriend, Larry Birkhead, he was being intimate with her lawyer, Howard K. Stern. They never discussed it again. And Jackie never met Larry face to face.

Jackie Hatten did speak to Larry Birkhead on the phone shortly after Daniel died. She told Larry, "I am worried about Anna, that she'll be next."

Without knowing what Jackie Hatten had seen, Anna's nannies, Quethlie Alexis and Nadine Alexie, accompanied by their attorney, told private investigators some details about Howard and Anna's home life. Howard, they said, was always on his computer and Anna often stayed in bed and watched movies. "Is there one video she loved watching?" an investigator asked.

"Yes," one of the nannies surprisingly said, "the one with Larry Birkhead and Howard . . . doing that thing."

"You mean like two gay guys?" the investigator asked. "Having sex?"

"Just like that," she nodded. The investigators were taken aback and told me that the nannies were clearly embarrassed about it, since they were quite religious.

"She'd lie in her bed and watch it," Nadine affirmed.

According to the nannies, she watched it over and over again.

March 2007

Under the direction of the Bahamas Court, Debra Opri was advised that Nassau Social Services was coordinating a social services evaluation concerning Larry Birkhead. Her Bahamian counterpart advised her to "get Larry ready" because a social services officer would be visiting Larry's house and would be looking at the kind of home and environment he would provide for his daughter.

When Opri told Larry that he needed to "child proof" his home, he asked her, "What do I do?" She asked whether he had done anything about getting a nursery ready. "Well," he replied, "Anna and I went shopping for a really nice nursery and we painted the baby's room pink."

Opri felt Larry was not up to the task and enlisted the help of a consultant, a former child services worker who knew the "checklist" for a social services inspection. On March 8, 2007, she met with Larry at his third floor, one bedroom apartment in Burbank, California. What she saw was filth—not acceptable to an adult, let alone a child—and said that the home had to be overhauled.

This is when Debra Opri learned about Byron—the "close friend" and "housemate" of Larry Birkhead's who had been living there with him for a while, rent free. Larry told her that Byron would help get the one-bedroom place ready.

But California social services told Larry that everyone who was going to be near Dannielynn, should she be awarded to him, would have to be fingerprinted and have a background check run. Larry suddenly panicked and said he did not, under any circumstances, want anyone to know about Byron.

Debra Opri became concerned with the "Byron issue." She asked whether Byron was going to be there when Dannielynn came, and Larry told her that he "would ask him to leave, but not now." The consultant repeated her concern about anyone with a questionable background and Opri told Larry that she was "not going to be part of any 'deception' with social services."

Larry Birkhead did not help in the cleaning of his house for social services. Instead, he just wanted to shop for and set up the nursery, and spend his time buying more and more baby clothes. When Opri, along with the social services consultant and an assistant, accompanied Larry to Babies 'R Us to get items for the nursery, they filled five shopping carts. At the register, Larry did not have the funds to pay for the purchases, which totaled $3,600. Once again, he turned to his attorney to foot the bill, saying he would pay her back. As of her June 7, 2007 filing, he had not.

Larry also did not help in childproofing the apartment with special hinges, locks, electrical covers, etc. That job was left to Mark Speer and his wife. The rugs were professionally cleaned, new sheets and towels purchased, and Larry's refrigerator and cupboards, which were full of spoiled and rotting food, were emptied and groceries purchased, again by Opri. She also, at his request, helped him find Dannielynn's new nanny, Roxie.

On the fourth day of house preparation, Debra Opri dropped by the apartment with a few final items. "You're getting too comfortable coming to our home all the time," Byron snapped at her. Larry refused to discuss Byron with her ever again after that weekend. But months later, within twenty-four hours of Opri's legal filing in which she mentioned Byron, Byron was suddenly asked by Larry to immediately get out, within the hour.

April 10, 2007

"I told you so," blond-haired, blue-eyed Larry Birkhead announced to the world after emerging triumphantly from the

Bahamian courthouse on April 10 with a big grin on his face. DNA expert Dr. Michael Baird had just confirmed to the court, "Essentially, he's the biological father," saying he was 99.99999 percent sure of it.

"I think Anna Nicole would have been proud that I fought it," Larry told the gathered press, who had waited outside the courthouse for the results. "Thank you for your support. Thank you for the people who got me this far. . . . Thank you very much. My baby's gonna be coming home pretty soon." Having recently parted ways with his U.S. attorney, he offered no thanks whatsoever to Debra Opri.

Howard K. Stern issued a statement following the dramatic DNA announcement, a statement that was a complete turnaround from all of his prior public statements and legal maneuvers which had dragged this case on for months. Now appearing to be Larry Birkhead's biggest supporter, he said he was "going to do whatever [he] can to make sure that he [Larry] gets sole custody."

Stunned and outraged, Virgie Arthur wanted to know why Howard suddenly dropped all legal blockades since at one point Howard told Larry he could drag this battle on in the courts for years. Howard threatened that the baby might be five years old before Larry would ever get her.

"What's up?" Virgie asked, cornering Larry Birkhead angrily in the courthouse hall. "What deal are you working?"

"I'm not doing anything," he said. "I just want to take my baby home."

"So, why is he suddenly helping you?" Virgie asked.

"He's just being nice." Larry said. Virgie said Birkhead was noticeably nervous, and was not able to look her in the eye.

Virgie told me later, "I knew he had cut a deal."

Alex Denk, Anna's former trainer, bodyguard and lover,

told me that shortly after Anna died he had an unusual conversation with Howard in which Howard asked him, "Remember Larry Birkhead had that relationship with the black male reporter before Anna?" Denk says he did remember that. In fact, before Anna got pregnant by Larry, she told Denk that Anna was attracted to Larry because "he has blonde hair, he's light-eyed," and, perhaps equally important, "Larry was gay and had dated a man before her." Denk, who told me he thought Howard had always been good to Anna, was shocked when he watched the Florida court proceedings. "I kept wondering why Howard didn't bring it [Larry being gay] up publicly in court, and I thought to myself, you sneaky bastard."

Denk was definitive that he thinks "Anna wanted to have a kid, but no attachment to a man. Larry was basically a sperm donor. He was not her boyfriend. She just wanted to have a baby with him and get rid of him." He says that now when he sees Larry Birkhead with the baby, "I feel like throwing up. That's not what she wanted. She did not want him to have the baby. It's very sad. It's opposite of what she wanted. Larry is an opportunist. . . . I was there when I heard Larry threaten her over the speakerphone, saying he'll go to the police. He wanted to get famous off of her. She was always worried about how any negative publicity would affect the Marshall case. Anna told me, 'He wants me to call the police on him, so he can get the headlines.'" Denk also said that Anna told him "that if anything ever happens to me, make sure he doesn't get the kid."

The night the DNA results were announced, Larry went to Horizons, now Howard K. Stern's Bahamian home, and took Howard up on his offer to "spend as much time with [Dannielynn] as he wants to right now." According to Virgie's team, Larry moved into the house with Howard for a month "to help in the transition." Larry gave the court as his address of record should they need to contact him in the next few weeks . . . Eastern Road. The Horizons house.

Meanwhile, Virgie Arthur had already filed paperwork asking to also be named as the child's guardian. "All I have ever cared about is the safety and well-being of my grand-daughter," Virgie told me at the time. Despite her anger behind the scenes, she tried to stay optimistic publicly. "I look forward to working with Larry to help raise and do what's best for Dannielynn."

The morning after the DNA results were announced, in his *Today Show* exclusive interview, Larry Birkhead said, "We might go from one fight to another, but I'm hoping that's not the case because, you know, there's only one dad, and I have no problem with anyone that has good intentions being allowed to visit the baby and see the baby and be a part of the baby's life."

He, however, said the idea of sharing custody "would imply that I'm unfit as a parent, which I'm not. . . . I'm looking forward to giving Dannielynn everything that she needs and all the love and support." Then, he talked about the Burbank "townhouse," the one that Debra Opri had helped him fix up. "She's got lots of toys and a nursery ready for her and she's got everything she's going to need . . . all I have to do is just give her the love and that's just what I'm ready and prepared to do."

May 1, 2007

Dannielynn Birkhead officially took off from Bahamian soil— where both her mother and brother were laid to rest—at 9:52 a.m. on May Day 2007. When the private jet carrying her, her father, and a TV crew from *Access Hollywood* touched down in Kentucky, her newly custodial father's home state, there was a swarm of media to welcome them. After shielding his baby from snapping paparazzi with his jacket, Larry Birkhead tucked his baby inside a waiting SUV and then went to greet the press. Larry Birkhead, former paparazzi and newly affirmed daddy, walked up to the airport's chain link fence to take questions from the hoard of waiting media with their cameras rolling and microphones hot.

Larry was momentarily overcome with emotion when he tried to describe the feeling of bringing his daughter home. He said, "It just feels good to be home," adding that he's ready to "relax and horse around"—an oddly appropriate turn of phrase considering it was the weekend of the Kentucky Derby, the event where he had originally met Dannielynn's mother, Anna Nicole Smith.

Asked where they were going to live, he said he was taking it "one day at a time." That this was just "one pit stop." Noticeably gaunt, Larry remarked he'd lost a lot of weight during the ordeal and said he was looking forward to eating "some home cooking." En route to his parents' Louisville home in the SUV, Roxie, the baby's new nanny, sang "Jesus Loves the Little Children." And Dannielynn smiled.

The following week, Larry Birkhead and Dannielynn made a splashy exclusive cover appearance in *OK! Magazine*. "Larry Birkhead once had a role on the TV soap opera *Passions*," the story began. "The last year of his life has had so much drama and intrigue that if a soap scriptwriter ever put it down on paper, the plot would likely be dismissed as too outlandish." For the privilege of telling the story of this soap opera and photographing "America's baby," *OK! Magazine* reportedly paid Larry Birkhead more than $1.5 million.

June 1, 2007

In his lawsuit filed in Los Angeles Superior Court against Debra Opri, Larry Birkhead claims fraud, legal malpractice, and breach of fiduciary duty, among other things. Larry claims that Opri falsely represented herself as a specialist in California family law.

Larry further alleged that Debra Opri spoke with others about business matters despite his requests otherwise and that she had started a "Save Dannielynn Fund" without his endorsement. Debra Opri, in her response, said that she was shocked to learn of the way he has treated not only her, but the many fans and supporters of his throughout this ordeal. She says that during the time of his litigation and mounting bills, Birkhead suggested to her to set up a legal fund to raise money. "But not too highly publicized so he wouldn't be obvious."

Her staff was instructed to get the paperwork ready and the publicity was started. The "Dannielynn Legal Fund" raised approximately $732 in donations that were sent in by the public in checks ranging mostly from one to twenty dollars. Opri's response claims that Larry would laugh at the small amounts, stating, "Oh, lookie here . . . a whole dollar." Gifts were also sent, and he'd discard most of them, only taking the things he thought he could use, like photo frames. "Occasionally, a fan would send $50 or more," Opri says, and she told him it was important to send thank you letters and keep a record. He said it wasn't worth his "time or signature" and the task was relegated to her staff.

Interestingly, Larry Birkhead's malpractice action against Debra Opri was filed by Michael Trope, originally of the Trope and Trope law firm, where Howard K. Stern's friend and secondary executor of Anna's will Ron Rale continues to work.

Opri was notified of this action on the first night of June at her residence. Who actually served her the legal papers? None other than John Nazarian, the well-known private investigator Howard K. Stern had sent to Jack Harding's house. Jack Harding, the man Daniel tried to hire to investigate Howard right before Daniel's death.

According to Opri, Nazarian told her to "be careful, they're out for your license" and that "an attorney's worst enemy is his client." Before he left, Nazarian also told Opri that he "felt bad for her" and wanted her to know that "Birkhead is a sick dude."

Soon after that, Opri learned that Nazarian made contact with one of her law clerks for the stated purpose of "squeezing him" to "turn on Opri" or "they would come after him and 'get him.'" Those threats were reported to authorities.

Opri charges that, "Birkhead, under the direction of Howard K. Stern, has filed this lawsuit against Opri for no other reason than to secure the remaining monies in his client trust fund, and not to pay Opri's bill."

She states bluntly: "All persons are connected in some way to Howard K. Stern and his increasingly growing involvement with and control over Birkhead, guardian of Dannielynn, heir to the Anna Nicole Smith estate, including the Marshall monies."

• • •

Despite the perceived deal, Virgie Arthur hoped she'd still at least be able to see her biological granddaughter when she arrived on U.S. soil. But weeks passed and Virgie Arthur had not been allowed to see Dannielynn. Larry Birkhead was not returning her calls and had not even sent Virgie so much as a photo of the baby, which she repeatedly asked for, so she could simply see what her granddaughter looks like. She had to settle with seeing the baby's growth, as the rest of the world did, on the front of *OK! Magazine*. Ironically, that was the same distant feeling Larry Birkhead had described to me in our first phone conversation. He told me he could only see his child by watching television.

Virgie Arthur's team still kept urging Larry Birkhead to put the millions he's receiving through media deals into a trust for the baby, and have an independent company monitor it. "You can live on it," Virgie said. "But don't squander it." After she told Larry that, she says he's only called her once in six weeks to "threaten her that if she doesn't drop the guardianship suit in the Bahamas, then he'll make sure the court fines her and have her pay for his legal fees and flights to and from the Bahamas."

Then, he told one of her representatives, "I have more money in my bank account than Virgie and her whole families' trailers are worth."

All that could be said back to Larry was, "What goes around, comes around."

CHAPTER 13

A Dramatic Ending

On March 26, 2007, in a press conference broadcast around the world, Seminole Police Chief Charlie Tiger and Broward County Medical Examiner Dr. Joshua Perper announced the results of the investigation into the death of Anna Nicole Smith. "We are convinced based on a thorough review of the evidence," Chief Tiger explained, "that this has been an accidental overdose with no other criminal element present."

Dr. Perper stepped up to the microphone to say her death was due to "combined drug intoxication" after taking a medley of chloral hydrate and at least eight other prescription drugs.

Chief Tiger said, "We have reviewed hundreds of hours of videotape captured by the hotel security cameras . . . and we found nothing unusual. We analyzed the contents of the laptop computer belonging to Mr. Stern, *with the approval of his attorney*, and we found nothing to indicate any foul play."

But did authorities have all the information they needed when they closed the case?

From the night before her death to the night after her death, there were numerous calls and frenetic activity that are now confirmed that raise new questions. The facts I have discovered in my investigation show a broad series of inconsistencies—outright untruths and questionable circumstances—which add to the mysterious death of Anna Nicole Smith.

• • •

After her death many ideas and theories have been floated about this story, some of which were pierced with reality, others brought down quickly with legal darts. But according to official documents and records, court transcripts, eyewitness accounts, and the participants' own words, here is the chain of events of what *definitely* happened during the key hours surrounding the death of Broward County Decedent No: 07-0223, Vickie Lynn Marshall.

The night before she died, February 7

5:13 p.m.
Howard received a call from Dr. Khris Eroshevich, Anna's psychiatrist and close friend. It was a seven-minute conversation. Dr. Khris left the Florida hotel that day for an evening flight to California.

6:38 p.m.
During the afternoon and evening, Howard called Ron Rale, Anna's attorney and Howard's longtime friend, at least five times. The last call to Rale that night was at 6:38 p.m.

6:41 p.m.

Howard received his final call of the evening on his cell phone from Alex Goen, CEO of Trimspa—a man in the middle of several lawsuits, including two class action suits against his company, both for false advertising. One of the suits named Anna Nicole, TrimSpa's spokesperson as a defendant.

Her weight loss may have been helped along by a variety of drugs and other products. Remember, when she died authorities noted she had an abscess on her left buttock. The boil had needle track markings and was filled with pus. This shot, Dr. Perper determined, was the genesis of her infection. Dr. Perper, however, never determined who actually gave her the shot. He also could not determine what was in it, as he was told it could have been either human growth hormone, vitamin B12, or immunoglobulin.

11:01 p.m.

Hotel surveillance footage captures a female, later identified as Melodie Delancy, entering Room 609. Room 609 was the adjoining room where Moe was staying over. Moe himself explained to Fox News that "It was an open room, and I knew she [Anna] wasn't feeling well." So, Howard asked Moe if he could stay over, and Moe told him, "Oh, no problem." According to the medical examiner's investigative report, Moe went to sleep in the guest room and "awakened around 4 a.m., at which time he checked the couch in the living room where he had seen her [Anna] when he came into the room. She was no longer there and he assumed she had gone to sleep in her room."

The Day Anna Nicole Smith Died, February 8

According to initial information obtained from Seminole Police Department detective Marian Bryant, Associate Medical Examiner Dr. Gertrude M. Juste reported in her scene investigation that Anna Nicole had stayed the prior night in suites 607 and 609 with her "significant other" Howard Stern and a friend after arriving from the Bahamas on Monday. "The decedent and Mr. Stern slept in room 607 and the friend (Maurice Brighthaupt, friend and bodyguard) slept in room 609."

There was no mention of Melodie Delancy's stay. But hotel surveillance cameras caught her leaving Room 609 at 8:03 a.m.

9:00 a.m.–9:30 a.m.

Moe said he went into Anna's room and "thought he saw her moving, but was not certain." He told Howard he was going down to meet his wife, Tas, for breakfast. Howard was now left alone in the suite with Anna.

10:00 a.m. and 10:03 a.m.

Howard used his cell phone to check his voicemail.

10:42 a.m.

Howard got a call from King Eric, who told him he was at the airport in Florida ready to be picked up. Seminole Detective Marian Bryant reported that: "At about 11:00 a.m. or 11:15 a.m., Mr. Stern spoke with the decedent [Anna] and informed her he was picking up guests from the airport."

But in actuality Howard did not go to the airport. He sent Moe.

217

10:45 a.m.

Howard called Moe who was having breakfast in the hotel with his wife. Tas told private investigators, "Howard wanted to stay with Anna because she was so sick." At 10:46 a.m. and 10:49 a.m., Howard checked his voicemail.

10:51 a.m.

Howard called Alex Goen of TrimSpa.

10:53 a.m.

Howard called Ron Rale. It is perhaps interesting to note it was still early in California, 7:53 a.m., where Rale lives.

10:54 a.m.

Moe called Goen Technologies.

10:56 a.m.–11:19 a.m.

There are several calls back and forth between Howard, King Eric, and Moe during Moe and Tas's drive to the airport to pick up King Eric, Brigitte, and King Eric's first mate.

Moe and Tas picked up the group and headed back to the Hard Rock Hotel with the Bahamian guests.

Around 11:50 a.m.

Howard walked down the hall and got in the elevator—leaving Anna in bed and completely alone. When the elevator doors opened in the lobby, Howard was greeted by Moe, Tas, King Eric, Brigitte, and the first mate. The group was just coming in to the hotel and about to head upstairs. According to both Tas and Moe's statements to private investigators, Howard was "acting strange." He was very "fidgety." Howard said rather peculiarly that he had to come to the lobby because his cell phone wasn't working in the room. Then, he turned around quickly and headed back up to the room with the newly arrived visitors.

11:54 a.m.
According to hall video surveillance footage, the party entered room 609 together. Howard walked up to the bedroom door where Anna was "not feeling well" and, according to his visitors shouted, "Anna, we have guests."

Brigitte said, "Don't wake her up." It also did not go unnoticed that Howard then made three phone calls on his cell phone. The cell phone that five minutes earlier he said wasn't working in the room.

The first of those calls was made at 11:59 a.m. Howard was calling the hotel liaison—*twice*—as she was almost simultaneously calling him. She would then call him back at 12:02, but he would already be on to his next call.

The hotel liaison is in charge of assisting V.I.P.s with their needs and helping them resolve any problems that might arise during their stay at the hotel. She was called many times during these critical minutes. She was close to Anna and her team. When Anna was in town for the January boxing match, for example, she bought Anna bras and helped her find a pink pair of boxing gloves.

Today's needs would be a bit more urgent . . . in fact they would be critical.

Noon
Howard called boat broker Mark Dekema, the gentleman who had sold Anna the boat the month before. According to both Dekema and the boat handyman, Howard had a 1 p.m. appointment at the marina, scheduled and confirmed. But when

the ten-minute phone call with Dekema ended, Howard immediately announced to his guests that he had to do something between 12 and 1 p.m.

"It's noon now," King Eric said.

"Then, he asked me if I could stay," Brigitte remembers. "Because they were 'going to go to the boat.' And I said, 'no problem.'"

Moe decided he didn't like the idea of Brigitte staying alone with Anna when she was so sick, so he asked Tas if she would mind hanging back too. "Just stay for a little while, baby," he asked. "Do you mind?"

Tas unenthusiastically agreed to stay.

According to information gathered by Seminole Police, the men went directly from the hotel to the boat and back.

12:14 p.m.
Howard, Moe, King Eric and the first mate exited Room 609 together. Moe left to do errands. King Eric and Howard headed to the Royal Palms Yacht Basin, leaving Tas and Brigitte in the suite with Anna in the bed. A hotel employee, who is familiar with the couple, told me that Howard had not left her side all week. The employee thought it was very "unusual" that Howard would not even be in the hotel when Anna was found dead, especially after her being so sick.

Tas also thought it was unusual that the room was so messy. The official scene investigation written later after Anna's body had been removed, described the mess like this: "Several white towels were strewn around on the bathroom floor and around the sinks. One of the sinks had what appeared to be caked yellow/brown residue of emesis [vomit] . . . The night table has various items, including cold medicine; and opened and non-opened cans of sodas; SlimFast; empty packs of gum and Nicorette; and an open box of Tamiflu tablets. The table on the right of the bed also contains a partly covered transparent glass jar containing a brownish liquid. There is a closet full of men's and women's clothes with multiple pairs of shoes littering the floor located to the left of the bedroom entrance. There was a pearl necklace on the foot of the bed and a Louis Vuitton purse on the chair by the window. Opposite the foot of the bed was an armoire-type of furniture against the wall with several drawers at the bottom, and a television set in the top portion. Some of the drawers were open and contained various articles of clothing."

12:17 p.m.
Howard made his second call to Mark Dekema. Though Dekema doesn't recall specifically what Howard asked during which phone conversation, he does remember Howard calling incessantly to discuss various things right before the appointment. Howard asked for directions, saying he was coming from the Hard Rock. He also asked if the work on the boat had been completed and Dekema says he gave Howard some ideas for where they could get boat supplies.

Howard called Mark Dekema five times between twelve and one o'clock.

12:27 p.m.
Moe called his wife Tas who was in the suite with Brigitte Neven.

12:44 p.m.
Tas called Moe. The call lasted one minute.

12:45 p.m.
Tas called Moe again immediately. This call lasted four minutes.

1:15–1:22 p.m.
Howard called boat broker Mark Dekema while he was with the boat handyman and King Eric at Royal Palms Yacht Basin. Dekema says Howard ended the call abruptly saying, "I have another call, I gotta take this." According to Dekema, he sounded a little urgent, a little desperate. But we now know that at that time, Howard didn't click over to another call. He would first check his voice mail (at 1:23 p.m.), and then he'd receive a call from Moe at 1:24.

1:17 p.m.
Tas called Moe. The call lasted a minute at the most.

1:19 p.m.
Tas called Moe back again. The call also lasted one minute.

1:22 p.m.
Moe called Tas. Their call lasted one minute.

1:23 p.m.
Howard called his voicemail.

1:24 p.m.
Moe called Howard. It was a one-minute call. Moe says that he told Howard to "get over there right away." Moe says Howard's response was "Oh, okay," then a few words more and then he clicked off.

So far, all parties involved have publicly suggested there

was only one call from Moe to Howard. In fact, here's how Moe described the sequence of events. Moe said: His wife called him, he called Howard, he called the hotel liaison, and "then I rushed back."

1:26 p.m.
Howard called Moe. It was a one-minute call.

1:27 p.m.–1:34 p.m.
For seven minutes Howard does not use his phone. The boat handyman says after Moe's call, Howard did not seem upset at all. He answered several questions, including the fact that he forgot to bring the handyman his few hundred dollars for the repairs. He then said in a monotone voice, "I have an emergency and have to leave."

The handyman said Howard "seemed very nonchalant when he said it. He didn't seem distressed . . . acted like it was a minor business issue versus a personal crisis." He walked back to his car. He didn't rush. Given what he knows now, the handyman said Howard's behavior was "extremely odd."

1:28 p.m.
Moe called his wife again. They spoke for four minutes. Tas said she had been trying in vain to resuscitate Anna.

1:31 p.m.
Moe called the hotel liaison on her cell. Almost simultaneously she was also calling him.

1:32 p.m.
Moe called the hotel liaison on her cell. The game of phone tag was on.

1:33 p.m.
Moe called the Hard Rock Gaming Commission Office, where the hotel liaison works.

1:33 p.m., 1:34 p.m., 1:35 p.m., 1:36 p.m.
Howard, now en route back to the hotel, called Moe over and over again.

1:34 p.m. and 1:36 p.m.
Moe called the hotel liaison.

1:36 p.m.
Moe called his wife Tas who was still in the room. 911 still has not been called.

1:36 p.m.
The hotel liaison called her boss, the Director of Operations. The Hard Rock Hotel was in a delicate situation.

1:37 p.m.
Howard made two calls to the hotel liaison back to back.

1:38 p.m.—Emergency services are finally called for.
911 cannot be called directly from a Hard Rock Hotel room phone, so Tas called a hotel operator, who in turn notified hotel security of the emergency.

1:38 p.m.
The hotel liaison called the Director of Operations, again.

1:39 p.m.
The hotel liaison called the office of the hotel's Director of Purchasing.

1:40 p.m.
Seminole Police dispatch received an emergency call from Hard Rock security.

1:40 p.m.
Moe entered Anna's room. Although Moe claimed he was in the room when 911 was initially called, he actually arrived two minutes later. He removed the covers and pulled Anna's naked body from the bed, and then he put her on the floor and began futile attempts at CPR.

1:43 p.m.
Hard Rock Hotel medical staff arrived to Room 607.

1:44 p.m.
The Seminole Police arrived to Room 607.

1:44 p.m.
The hotel liaison called Howard.

1:47 p.m.
Seminole Fire Rescue arrived to Room 607, as does Hollywood, Florida, Fire and Rescue.

1:48 p.m.
The hotel liaison called Howard's cell phone again.

1:51 p.m.
Howard entered the room. Tas said, "He had no reaction at first, he was unemotional."

Paramedics asked Howard, "How long has she been like this?" and "What was she taking?" According to Tas, Howard answered, "I don't know. I don't know."

Howard then called Dr. Khris, who was back in California.

1:54 p.m.
Howard called Dr. Khris, who prescribed all nine medications found in Anna's system when she died, including the chloral hydrate, which was prescribed to Howard Stern.

1:59 p.m.
Seminole Police Detectives arrived on the scene. Howard told Seminole Police, "that he did not see her take medication, but believed she was taking her medication."

2:02 p.m. and 2:09 p.m.
Howard called Dr. Khris again. The female doctor told paramedics on the phone that Anna had been taking medication since experiencing problems with her breast implants and recently for depression over her son's death.

2:09 p.m.
Dr. Khris called the Hard Rock Hotel liaison.

Approximately 2:15 p.m.
Anna was wheeled out of the Hard Rock Hotel, Howard followed the gurney to the hallway elevator, but then stayed upstairs as Moe left with Anna to the hospital. Howard was seen crouching down in the hallway, with his hands covering his face.

2:27 p.m., 2:30 p.m., 2:32 p.m.
Howard repeatedly called Moe.

2:31 p.m.
Dr. Khris called the hotel liaison.

2:36 p.m.
The hotel liaison called the hotel's Director of Operations.

2:37 p.m.
Alex Katz called the liaison. He was the other person in the room with them Monday night after they arrived, the night Anna had the 105-degree fever. The same person who an eyewitness says picked up medication for Anna prescribed in his name.

2:43 p.m.
The ambulance carrying Anna Nicole Smith arrived at Memorial Regional Hospital.

2:49 p.m.
Anna Nicole Smith was pronounced dead.

3:12 p.m.
Howard called Alex Goen of TrimSpa.

3:13 p.m.
Howard called the Hard Rock Hotel's main number.

3:14 p.m.
Howard called Alex Goen of TrimSpa.

3:17 p.m.
Alex Goen called Howard.

3:21 p.m.
Howard called the Horizons house in the Bahamas.

3:23 p.m.
Howard got a call from the Boesch Law Firm, which handles Anna's case against J. Howard Marshall's family.

3:37 p.m. and 3:38 p.m.
Howard called attorney Ron Rale.

3:48 p.m.–3:52 p.m.
Ron Rale was live with me on MSNBC, officially breaking the news that "Anna Nicole is deceased." He said on the air that Howard is "obviously speechless," "unable to speak."

3:49 p.m. and 3:51 p.m.
Howard wasn't quite speechless. He called *Entertainment Tonight*/Paramount and spoke with them first for two minutes, then for four minutes. According to eyewitnesses, he quickly reserved a block of rooms for the *Entertainment Tonight* crew. Host Mark Steines would be flying in that night on the *ET* jet with Dr. Khristine Eroshevich.

4:15 p.m.
Howard got a call from Alex Goen of TrimSpa.

4:26 p.m.
Howard called Ray Martino in California (where Anna's son Daniel used to live).

4:27 p.m.
Howard called the hotel liaison.

4:34 p.m.
Howard called the hotel liaison again.

4:47 p.m.
Hotel liaison called Howard twice.

4:49 p.m.
Howard called "information."

4:51 p.m. and 4:52 p.m.
Howard called a local elementary school and then its aftercare program.

4:55 p.m.
The hotel liaison called Howard.

4:59 p.m.
Anna Nicole's body arrived at the Medical Examiner's office and is logged in.

5:38 p.m.
Leon Stern, Howard's father, called Howard.

7:12 p.m. and 7:13 p.m.
Moe called Ron Rale.

8:25 p.m.
Seminole Police Detectives cleared the scene.

•   •   •

Although the coroner has never given an exact time of death, the last person to see Anna alive was, according to his own comments to police, Howard K. Stern. But Howard is quick to point out that he wasn't the one to discover her body. In fact, he made an unusual comment to a close friend that "He is tormented by Anna's death and felt if he was the one who found her body, after being there during Daniel's death, he would've killed himself too. That the pain of finding her, after what happened with Daniel, would've been too much for Howard."

Detectives found eleven prescription medications in various places in the suite, including the nightstand, the dresser drawer, and especially in Howard's now infamous duffel bag. The bag was found on the floor and was full of prescription medicine mostly written to Howard. Among the medications found in Howard's duffel bag was chloral hydrate, considered by Dr. Perper to be "the most significant drug implicated in this fatality."

Moe told private investigators he felt guilty, wondering if what was inside the packages of prescriptions he received at his house and delivered to Howard on that Monday night before her death, was what killed Anna. Moe also told numerous people he was put under intense pressure "not to talk" and to "shut his wife up." Howard and his attorneys were calling Moe, telling him to "stay in our camp." Moe felt so much stress that he was hospitalized at least twice. His tell-all book, *Baby Girl*, which was supposed to give, among other things, a "candid look at Smith's ability to manipulate her men, her depression after the death of her son, and her drug use" was cancelled before publication.

Howard, Ron Rale, and Larry Birkhead called Moe relentlessly after his book deal was announced. Larry was concerned about what Moe was going to write about him in the book, and Ron Rale and Howard kept telling Moe "to keep Tas quiet." Moe believes Howard's team "played a role in killing his book deal."

There may be more concerns weighing heavily on Moe.

After Anna's death, Moe presented his story on Fox News, and said he had been gone "like fifteen minutes" from the hotel room when he called to check on how Anna was doing. He did call his wife at 12:27 p.m., approximately fifteen minutes after he left the room. But what happened before hotel surveillance cameras have him arriving back at 1:40 p.m., is a bit strange and is still confusing.

"Initial comments and initial reactions are often the most telling in a case," former New York Police Department squad commander Joe Cardinale told me, speaking about cases in general.

Indeed, the initial scene investigation as documented by Seminole Detective Marian Bryant, states something both interesting and perplexing. "Around 12:30 p.m., the bodyguard's wife checked on the decedent and observed her to be blue. She immediately called her husband, Maurice Brighthaupt, and informed him of the situation. She also started CPR in her capacity as a registered nurse. As soon as Maurice returned to the hotel, he immediately called the Seminole Emergency Medical Personnel around 1:40 p.m."

From 12:27 p.m. to 1:40 p.m. is obviously not "immediately." It is also interesting to note that both Moe and his wife initially referred to 12:30, or about fifteen minutes after Moe left the room.

Tas said when she spoke to Moe on the phone, "I don't like what I'm seeing. Anna has purple splotches on her face and body. She's not breathing and looks blue."

"Blue?" Moe asked.

Dr. Howard Adelman, former Deputy Chief Medical Examiner for Suffolk County, New York, said the purple splotches that Tas described on Anna's face is "because the blood is not oxygenating. They could appear as soon as three to four minutes after someone dies. Soon after the heart stops beating, you begin to see these."

"When I blew into her, I heard a gurgling sound," Tas remembered. "I told Moe I knew it was not good."

Tas "knew the gurgling sound was the sound you hear after people are already dead." She told private investigators, "I've seen many dead people. That's what happens when people are settling." She believes "Anna was already dead for some time" and even suggested that "Anna may have been dead for several hours." In fact, Tas recently confided to private investigators that, looking back, she now remembers "Anna's skin color didn't look right" when she first walked in the room, but she "didn't put it together until Brigitte looked closely at Anna later."

Brigitte Neven, the woman who found Anna's lifeless body and brought it to Tas's attention, told me Anna's body was still warm, which forensics experts say does not necessarily mean she just died. "She could've been dead anywhere from a few minutes up to twelve hours," Dr. Adelman said. "Because she was wrapped in a heavy bed cover, her body could remain warm for three to four hours after she died. She had a 105-degree fever on Monday. Even if it dropped to 100 degrees on Tuesday, it could've spiked back up to 105 degrees or higher before she died, especially if she had an infection. Such a high fever right before death, as well as her being insulated in a heavy blanket, could cause her body to stay warm to the touch for up to twelve hours. It takes time for someone's temperature to drop, especially if they are wrapped in a warm blanket." Remember, Anna was found cocooned head to toe in a down comforter and duvet cover.

It was also many minutes or more until medical help was contacted. When private investigators asked Tas how as a nurse she could let so much time pass before 911 was called, she said, "I don't know. I just thought to call my husband. I was panicking."

Moe said that after the initial call from his wife, there were no other calls between them before he got back to the room. This is false as there was a flurry of calls between all the parties, yet incredibly, no calls directly to 911. Remember that the reason Moe says he didn't call 911 directly was that his cell phone was registered to a different county in Florida and because he claimed he did not know the address of the Hard Rock, a place he'd been to frequently.

• • •

Tas said she was shocked that Dr. Perper asked her only a few questions: "Did you give Anna any medications?" "What did you see?" and "Did you see her move?" Dr. Perper didn't talk to Brigitte Neven according to his own report, and she was the woman who actually first found Anna unconscious.

A few other things have bothered Tas since that horrible day. When they all went into the room at 11:54 a.m. the morning Anna died, she says Howard did something that seemed calculated. He positioned his body between the two rooms in such a manner that his visitors—King Eric, Brigitte, and Tas—had a blocked view into Anna's bedroom. She also thought it was strange that Howard didn't want to leave Anna to go pick up King Eric and Brigitte at the airport, but then suddenly soon after that, left Anna to go look at the boat.

She also made a surprising discovery. When she sat in one of two chairs at the foot of Anna's bed to work on the computer, she noticed Howard's computer was on and open on the floor to the right of the chair. A $37,000 wire transfer he had made that morning was still illuminated on the screen. Tas says she was on the phone with Moe when she saw the wire transfer message. (Police did check Howard's computer for e-mails sometime after her death, but were not informed of any wire transfers and therefore did not check for any.) Both the boat broker and handyman know of no large amount like this that would have been associated with the boat.

Perhaps most disconcerting was that there was a baby bottle positioned on top of Anna with the same orange-brown residue in it as the jug on the nightstand. The contents of both the baby bottle and the jug were tested and it turned out to be Pedialyte, an oral electrolyte maintenance solution, specially formulated for children with diarrhea and vomiting. Tas said the baby bottle bothered her very much. It wasn't the contents that troubled her. She believes "the baby bottle was planted . . . if Anna was truly just sleeping, it would've fallen off the minute she moved because of the strange position it was in." The baby bottle was lying slanted on Anna's shoulder and neck on top of the covers. "There's no way she put it there herself."

• • •

In addition, Dr. Khris Eroshevich has cause for concern, which may be why she refused to talk to Seminole Police. To have someone under your medical supervision with a raging 105-degree temperature and not take her to the hospital is deadly dangerous. "The only adults I have seen with a fever of 105 degrees are suffering from heat exhaustion/heat stroke, are extraordinarily ill, or near death," Dr. Keith Eddleman told me. His practice at Mt. Sinai Hospital in New York City sees more than 17,000 patients a year. "That is an astronomically high fever, seizure range. If someone arrives at the hospital with that high of a temperature, it's a medical emergency. You summon everybody to get that body temperature down. As a doctor, to not seek emergency care for one of your patients with a 105-degree temperature, you are asking for medical malpractice problems."

Add this to the laundry list of prescription drugs Dr. Khris provided for Anna under numerous names, and one can see why the California Medical Board and the Federal Drug Enforcement Administration opened an investigation into Dr. Khris.

Fox News quoted Dr. Chip Walls, a forensic toxicologist for the Miller School of Medicine at the University of Miami, who said chloral hydrate is rarely prescribed and is known to be fatal if combined with certain other drugs—including the sedative Lorazepam, which the autopsy showed Anna was taking, also given to her by Dr. Khris. "It's very toxic if you mix it with any other central nervous system depressant drugs," Walls said. "You could get profound sedation leading up to coma and respiratory arrest."

Though Dr. Khris refused to talk to Seminole Police, she was willing to talk to *Entertainment Tonight*. In fact, as the *Entertainment Tonight* crew, including host Mark Steines, boarded a plane to fly to Florida the night of Anna's death, Dr. Khris joined them. "When the news broke of Anna's death—I truly didn't believe it," Mark Steines wrote on his Internet blog. "We were all quite literally crushed when we were told the news by people close to Anna. I immediately boarded a plane to Florida along with Khristine Eroshevich, Anna's close confidant, who got me up to speed on the last moments of Anna's life. She told me who was there, what Howard was going through and why the paternity battle Anna had been suffering through was literally too much for her to bear."

It seemed as if Dr. Khris—like other "Anna close confidants," including Howard K. Stern, Alex Goen, and Ron Rale—

was already positioning Anna's death as a suicide, or at least tied to her depression. In fact, I am aware that both Dr. Khris and Howard tried to convince Dr. Perper that Anna committed suicide, even before the autopsy was completed.

Howard's family meanwhile rallied around to defend Howard and suggest that Anna's drug use was only facilitated by Anna. "He was in love with her, why would he kill her?" Howard's sister, Bonnie Stern, was quick to tell *People* magazine after Anna's death. "My brother never fed her a drug in her life. Never! Howard couldn't control the situation. It was up to Anna. When someone wants to do something, you can't stop it."

Life After Death

Less than twenty-four hours after her death, Anna Nicole's Bahamian home, Horizons, was "broken into" and digital photos and home videos were taken, many of which, according to Ron Rale, were "extraordinarily personal in nature." Within days of her tragic demise, photos of Anna lying on a bed with Bahamian immigration minister Shane Gibson emerged in the media. Although both of them were fully clothed, they were gazing into each other's eyes with their faces just inches apart. It was enough to force his resignation. Then, before the circus-like trial over custody of her body was over, the infamous "clown" video Howard made of Anna in an obviously impaired state made its debut.

And it's only gotten even more peculiar from there.

Back in the Bahamas, something interesting happened the morning of Anna's death at the five-bedroom house she had bought in December and was remodeling on the opposite end of the island from the Horizons house. The new house, in an area known as Coral Harbor, was being gutted as well as having exterior cosmetic modifications done in Anna's favorite shade of pink. Neighbor Keshlia Lockhart had been watching the work progress and had been told by King Eric, who told her he had hired the crews, that Howard and Anna had plenty of money allotted for all the renovations.

Keshlia Lockhart's impression was that the renovations would take about three months to do. Every morning, approximately ten construction men had been working on the house for several weeks each day from 7:30 a.m. until four or four-thirty. In the week before Anna's death, they started spraying the outside of the house with a stucco type material. Anna wanted to change the light pink outside to a darker pink. They hadn't finished the spray job and had been there the day before, doing a typical day's work.

But interestingly they did not show up the morning of the day Anna died, and have not been back since. Keshlia Lockhart thinks the timing of that is strange. She also says the lights in the house remained on for months.

Cracker Ltd., the same company that bought the house, also bought Anna's boat. The Bahamian company was formed specifically for that purpose according to one of Howard K. Stern's attorneys, Wayne Munroe. Munroe told me that there are only two shareholders and directors for Cracker Ltd.— him and his associate attorney, Dion Smith. Dion Smith is the man who put his official signature on Dannielynn's birth certificate, which lists Howard K. Stern as the father.

On the Saturday morning after Anna's death at approximately 7 a.m., Mark Dekema says he went for supplies and had breakfast with King Eric, Brigitte, and their first mate. He says around 10:30–11 a.m. King Eric passed the phone to Dekema to talk to Howard. Dekema asked Howard if he wanted to reconsider dealing with the boat right now after such a terrible loss. Dekema said under the circumstances, he'd understand if Howard decided that he didn't feel like caring for the boat anymore and would now want to sell it, which Dekema said he'd be happy to help him do. Howard told him his plans had not changed with the boat at all. King Eric would be taking it to Nassau right away.

Dekema also asked Brigitte what happened to Anna the day she died. "She collapsed," Brigitte told him. Dekema was genuinely surprised when I informed him that Anna was found dead while sleeping in her bed.

• • •

In June 2007, Larry Birkhead moved into Anna's house in Los Angeles, the one right next door to Dr. Khristine Eroshevich. And he did not contest Howard being the executor of Anna's estate.

A mutual friend of both Larry Birkhead and Howard K. Stern says he believes they reached a deal on behalf of Dannielynn and "on behalf of the almighty dollar." Regarding Anna's estate, he said, "Friends do not believe for a second that Anna only had ten thousand dollars in cash and seven hundred thousand dollars in assets [her Los Angeles house]." They wonder what happened to all the expensive jewelry Anna received from J. Howard Marshall, among other things. They believe the money is elsewhere in offshore accounts and with other companies, and friends have apparently warned Howard and Larry, "Whatever you do and say amongst yourselves, Dannielynn is going to know about it one day. Larry has America's baby now and everyone feels they have a stake in her."

Former foes Larry Birkhead and Howard K. Stern sat side-by-side in a courtroom in June 2007 as Superior Court Commissioner Mitchell L. Beckloff admitted Anna Nicole Smith's July 30, 2001, will into probate. He ordered that Larry Birkhead, father of the late model's young daughter, would be guardian of the estate while Howard K. Stern would serve as the executor of her will.

Gorgeous little Dannielynn, America's newest cover-girl, stands to possibly inherit millions from the estate of her mother's late husband, Texas oil tycoon J. Howard Marshall II.

In an impromptu news conference, Stern and Birkhead took a moment to stand, once again, in the media spotlight. This time they announced they were on good terms, and that both of them were concerned for the welfare of Dannielynn and will do everything necessary to assure a good future for her.

"I'm going to help Larry any way I can," Howard said. "Larry will be a good father."

"I have another new title today," Larry said, smiling. "In addition to father, I'm guardian. So it's a very good day." He added that he'd had a wonderful Father's Day with his daughter. "It's one I will remember."

"Right now, Dannielynn is the most famous baby in America," Howard said. "Maybe five years from now it won't be that way and she can just be a normal little girl." I remembered what Mark Speer, Larry's former security detail, recounted about Larry's hope that he'd make another million dollars off the rights to the first photo of him and Dannielynn before she turned eighteen.

Mark Speer is also skeptical about Larry and Howard's apparent "friendship." "There is no way after what I heard firsthand at the Bahamian police station and at Howard's house, no way Larry Birkhead would even be civil to him unless he's in cahoots with him and has a deal." Moe Brighthaupt has also told people he knows that Howard struck a deal with Larry Birkhead.

Virgie Arthur said, "J. Howard is dead. My grandson is dead. Now, my daughter is dead. That money is tainted for any greedy person that grabs it." And Virgie says that so far the prospect of that money has brought her family nothing but grief. She told me she "thinks about Ron Goldman's family in the O.J. Simpson case all the time. I see how much pain they are still going through, and I think that's what my life will now be like."

• • •

Unlike her over-the-top life, Anna Nicole Smith went out of the world quietly, without so much as a whimper. Anna told friends and relatives that she always thought she'd die young like her idol Marilyn Monroe. When she did so, she too was found naked like Marilyn of an apparent drug overdose. But Jackie Hatten says Anna never believed Marilyn's death was a suicide. "I don't think Marilyn Monroe killed herself," Anna told Jackie. "She was murdered."

"It's like bad fiction," *Playboy* founder Hugh Hefner told me. "As tragic as it was, in another sense, it is the life and the end that she might have written for herself." Regarding Anna's passing, he said, "There was obviously some drug abuse there, both prescription and presumably non-prescription. But I also think that one of the tragedies of her life is some bad choices in terms of friends and associates."

Hugh Hefner remembers, "I think that she was always a very sincere person, and made some unfortunate choices. But, a good, good person—a small town girl with big dreams. And,

I think that is the key to why she was so fascinating to so many people. It is easy to identify with her."

And people continue to flock to all things Anna Nicole. Her home in the Bahamas has turned into a "Graceland" of sorts, with a constant line of tourists passing by her house and also visiting her grave as fans have for years visited Marilyn's. Bahamian taxi drivers have made fliers to promote their "Anna tour" around the island, often charging twenty dollars per tourist off the cruise ships they drive out to the house. The luxury suite where she died at the Hard Rock was completely refurbished, renumbered, and has been "spiritually cleansed" by a Native American Indian shaman. Fans have been desperately trying to book a night in the room where she took her last breath.

Everything surrounding the story of Anna Nicole Smith's death seems a bit too unreal to be real, almost as if it is indeed an episode of a made-for-TV docudrama. Unfortunately, Dannielynn Hope Birkhead is forever without her mother. Anna Nicole is dead, lying beneath foreign soil, next to her son, Dannielynn's brother, who had just come for a short visit to celebrate her birth.

Her father, Larry Birkhead, is filled with ambition. My hope is that his ambition doesn't overtake the future of Anna Nicole's little girl.

Acknowledgments

I AM GRATEFUL FOR THE THOROUGH SCOPE, EXAMINATION, AND support of law enforcement officers—local, state, and federal—who provided tremendous assistance to me with this project, some of whom I've had the pleasure of working with for many years in my career. I also want to thank the paramedics and forensic experts whose review of their own and others' reports helped me untangle the medical web of perplexing issues that surrounded us as this story unfolded.

For almost two decades, the knowledge, insight, and cross-references of these professionals have helped me separate fact from fiction, evidence from perception, and knowledge from speculation. To this day, their contributions remain an invaluable cornerstone to my work. For their unwavering commitment and dedication to justice, I am forever in their debt.

Realizing this is a controversial book, I must remember what my old journalism professor Dr. Lee Dudek taught me years ago. He said journalism is not a passive business. A reporter's job is to question the answers and actions, especially when intent and motivations may be hidden or unclear, and demand a voice.

My hope is that this book will serve to "connect the dots," provide solid facts in this captivating case, and finally "break the dam of fiction" regarding what really happened to Anna Nicole Smith and what she wanted for her precious little girl.

I also hope Anna's story will serve as a lesson to us all to be mindful of our friends, careful about our physical well-being, and supportive of those around us who need to conquer their addictions before those addictions consume and, sadly, conquer them.